THE
COLLEGE
LABYRINTH

A MINDFUL
ADMISSIONS APPROACH

Dr. Erin Avery, CEP

Print ISBN: 978-1-09830-027-2

eBook ISBN: 978-1-09830-028-9

PRAISE FOR THE COLLEGE LABYRINTH

Erin Avery is an educator and a writer who lives for the soul, or more accurately stands for the defense of the soul of students seeking the opportunity of college.

We collectively have created and embraced the madness of the 21st century college admissions in America, and along the way we have contorted the art and experience of education, the creativity and passion of our students, and the very notion of adolescence itself. Avery provides a series of steps to relieve the madness and return schools to the most noble expression of their mission.

Tad Roach, Head of School, St. Andrew's School, DE

There are hundreds of guide books that address the 'magic elixir' needed to gain admission to a competitive college. On the other end of the spectrum, Dr. Erin Avery's "College Labyrinth," encourages the reader to question and explore their own journeys of self-discovery as they assess their higher educational values and needs. Dr. Avery has organized her book with the intention of educating families on the many issues surrounding college admissions in the 21st century. Her call to authenticity and honesty in the process is refreshing and should be a must-read for families who are going through the college search and application process. This book will also give educators valuable insights in guiding their students.

Nicole Oringer, MA, M.Ed., CollegeWise

While immersed in our technological world, the college application process no longer resembles how previous generations tackled their application journey. Therefore, families and professionals need to take a keen look at this transition in a new light. Dr. Avery's book will bring us into a new and enlightened journey. While this immense undertaking is still a rite of passage, Dr. Avery brings in three strong elements within the process: self-reflection, self-discovery, and mindfulness in order to maintain comfort with this next phase of life. These three pieces are paramount in maintaining a balance not only in this process, but as lifelong lessons.

Sandy Furth, MS, CEP, World Student Support

Over the last three decades the college admissions process has moved from a hope-filled educational decision to a journey fraught with anxiety for many high school students and their families. How did we get here? Dr. Avery explores this adolescent developmental dynamic with compassion, deep understanding, and pragmatic and proven advice. She challenges us to realign the paradigm: to explore the reasons behind increased pressure and anxiety, and to become educated around both healthy habits of self-assessment and the realities of college admissions that super-sized media headlines ignore. An important book for families and professionals alike at a critical time in American higher education, Dr. Avery's approach is a welcome guiding companion.

Katelyn Gleason Klapper, Certified Educational Planner
Commission Chair, American Institute of Certified
Educational Planners

ACKNOWLEDGEMENTS

I express such immeasurable gratitude to my husband, Charlie.

To my mentor, Dr. Dan Kroger, who has become for me what I strive to be for my own students.

To my beloved parents who have encouraged me along the path, I am grateful to you for inculcating in me the invaluable gift of my faith, a love for music, and compassion for those in need. I simply could not have accomplished this without your support.

To Jenna McAteer, my colleague to whom I owe an inordinate amount of thanks. Truly, your tireless work to round the rough edges of this undertaking has been humbling to me. To Jill Kimberley Hartwell Geoffrion, who led me on a pilgrimage back to love, patience, passion, observation and healing. A special thank you to Sadie Britton who sat with me with open manuscripts and open minds to what this book might be. Thanks also to Michael McIrvin who uses words as prisms to create color out of chaos.

Finally, to Steve Antonoff, educator, mentor and colleague, who donates myriad hours annually to elevating the field of educational consulting, and who encouraged me to lend my voice and perspective to this topic, I cannot thank you enough for your student-centered inspiration.

FOREWORD

Planning for college ought to be a time of celebrating successes, recognizing vulnerabilities, and looking forward to a new, exciting phase of life. For many students and families, however, the college admission process has become a toxic slog, clouded by uncertainty, stress, and second-guessing. The atmosphere that surrounds today's college selection process calls to mind one of those long slow-moving airport walkways where there's no getting off until the bitter end. Many high-school juniors and seniors on the college admission moving walkway feel stuck, frustrated, anxious to make it to their destination, yet scared to arrive. And if that destination isn't one of their "dream" colleges, they arrive unhappy. They arrive feeling they aren't as "good" as a classmate. They arrive feeling like losers before their journey has even begun.

Erin Avery offers an antidote to this scenario. Through a combination of Greek mythology, spirituality, mindfulness, Chinese philosophy, sound educational theory, and just plain common sense, Dr. Avery exposes the flaws inherent in today's college planning and provides concrete alternatives to help make college selection a transformative journey for both students and families.

Dr. Avery's suggestions are specific and substantive, but it is her wisdom that makes *The College Labyrinth* a must-read. As a certified educational planner, Dr. Avery lives the college admission process every day in her work with students and parents. Building on her experience, she provides an optimistic but also realistic roadmap to a calmer, student-directed, transition from high school to college.

Over the course of my own career in college admissions and selection, I have become ever more concerned that college planning is causing students to burn out. I worry that grades are valued over learning, that high school is seen only as a route to the "right" college and that few students dare to consider new opportunities or explore unfamiliar subjects that won't add prestige to an application or boost a GPA. I worry that cramming for standardized tests, texting nonstop, and squandering hours on electronic devices have reduced precious time available for real connection with people and for engagement in national and international discussions. I worry that mental health is being sacrificed in order to gain a competitive admission edge. For too many high school students, their sense of self is wholly dependent on doing everything perfectly. They forget that it's the imperfections of life that make us strong. Stumbling and picking yourself up is essential to learn resiliency and problem-solving.

Is getting into a highly competitive college worth sacrificing growing, learning, and self-discovery in high school? I don't think so, and neither does Erin Avery. In *The College Labyrinth*, she offers tools and strategies for moving through this process with sanity. She invites students to get off that frustrating college admission walkway and take a journey of self-discovery instead. Under her tutelage, students are guided to look at college planning as a "sacred journey" and even a "pilgrimage." She challenges college planners to "search for the right places, not necessarily the best places."

In this perceptive and practical guide, Dr. Avery shares valuable insights into decision-making, self-exploration, family expectations, the influence of social media on college planning, the over-rewarding of children, and the true definition of the "dream college." She leads her readers toward "humanizing this vulnerable process" of college search and selection—a humanization that is much needed.

The Avery Approach is based on Erin Avery's research, experience as a college advisor, and countless hours of pondering ways to make college selection a smoother and more fulfilling process. Her approach introduces the reader to tactics and strategies such as self-centering, the labyrinth, and the value of mindfulness in college planning. She defines and underscores the importance of such concepts as "recruit to reject," "deconstructing the stressors," "dis-orientation," "launching into the liminal," "deep peace," and "seekers with intense spiritual yearning." She even offers some practical suggestions on how to save the college selection system from itself.

Erin Avery is my colleague and friend. I also consider her a student of mine and have watched with great pride as she has grown as an able, thoughtful educational consultant over the past two decades. We have taught the same courses for college advisors, and our views often merge. But I'm most proud to say that at this point in my career, I am learning from her. Readers of this book will also benefit from her experience and knowledge. What's more they will find themselves armed with a new attitude toward identifying and getting into a great college while still preserving the joys of adolescence.

—Steven R. Antonoff

TABLE OF CONTENTS

PART ONE: THE JOURNEY IN

This may appear merely to be a book about college admission, but do not be deceived. It is also a sacred journey. It involves adolescents with large hearts longing for the imagination of which many have been strip-mined in the name of achievement. This is also a path that spirals upward and outward. Be prepared to be invited to look heavenward, even, and especially, if your spirituality is defined by the beauty of the view, and to look outward at how you can impact the young people in your life. Be cautious only in the sense that you will be ushered into a narrow space, but trust that there is only one path and no dead ends. There indeed may be monsters awaiting you, however they may simply be projections of your own deep inner work waiting to be greeted and released. Befriend those that you encounter; they will provide a unique brand of filial love in the form of *communitas*. Finally, be at peace in the space that follows. We call it liminal space. Your teenagers are already in there awaiting you. So pause, remove or release whatever you must to acknowledge holy ground. Welcome to your center.

CHAPTER ONE

Admissions Transitions

An independent educational consultant for the better part of two decades, I co-journey with adolescents on their passage from high school to college. Clients climb the stairs to my office, the stairwell, walls and waiting room ablaze with the colors of college pennants I have received from previous clients or collected from my own myriad campus visits—symbols of the destinations my current clients hope to reach. Bright mugs from various institutions of higher learning line the ledges of my office, and these too represent the acceptance my clients have enjoyed and hope to achieve. Each day these young students join me to complete personality inventories, fill out probing college-match questionnaires, edit essays, or debrief about recent campus tours and information sessions; and at the outset of our journey together, nearly every one of them displays one or more of what I think of as symptoms of their misunderstanding of the process in which we are engaged: disorientation, confusion, fear, vulnerability, and being overwhelmed. Rather than viewing the college application process as a prize to be won, from the outset, we attempt to assert that the process is inherently what these feelings gesture at: a journey of self-discovery. Because most teens assume it has to be a zero-sum game, fraught with stress, competition and struggle, of course their preconceptions of the process are pejorative. But when we cast the process as a decision tree with small, deliberate steps, it becomes much more manageable, and the emphasis becomes the student him/herself and not the school.

I work one-on-one with my clients and their stakeholders (parents and step-parents, grandparents, or other guardians), and the above list contains just some of the negative emotions applicants and their respective stakeholders express to me at the outset of the process, emotions that have also surfaced in my field research into the perception of students regarding their transition to college. As a result, I include questions of self-exploration in my consultations in order to help them reorient their perspective from an overemphasis on name-brand universities to one that emphasizes the student's interests, strengths and academic and extracurricular aspirations. Questions include: Do you enjoy reading? Do you want to have access to cultural offerings at or near your college? Do school spirit and spectator sports matter to you? How do you feel about Greek life? What is your leadership style? Do you have any strong opinions about how best you learn? Are you learning something about yourself during this process that allows you to see beyond the immediate goal of application completion?

The larger goal is to help them determine how their desire to attenuate the discomfort of the unknown denies them an invaluable opportunity for growth as they walk this unfamiliar path. In fact, that is an important element of this book: an exploration of how the stressful landscape of college costs and selective admission forces students to view the college process as a race rather than a sacred journey, which it can be if undertaken with the right guidance. I will argue that this contemporary rite of passage can be viewed as an opportunity for young people to learn about and understand themselves. In fact, the process as sacred journey not only allows them to develop their own sense of themselves at this young age relative to the world at large but allows them to engage deeply with what it is to be human within the overall epic journey that is their life. Readers, whether students or their stakeholders, will be encouraged to develop an increased sense of comfort with the unknown that is inherent in the admissions process, even view it as an adventure and an integral part of the process of self-discovery.

I believe that knowledge of self—a key component of the college admissions process that is also important in our respective life journeys—must originate in the practice of self-centering, which means exploring one's internal landscape and grounding one's sensibilities from within, no easy task in our postmodern moment and all its attendant pressures on the individual from without. Currently, overemphasis on college as the only goal of students' academic outcomes collides with social media's tendency to turn individuals into consumers constantly looking outward for affirmation and answers (as in an Instagram survey on whether to buy the blue shirt or the red shirt). Consequently, in this book I will encourage college admissions stakeholders to shift teens' attentiveness toward their inner compasses and to provide tools to help applicants remain centered.

In the chapters that follow, applying Victor and Edith Turner's research on pilgrimage, in particular the concepts of liminality (the experience of abiding in a state of transition) and *communitas* (openness to forming tight relationships while encountering liminality with others in the midst of a like journey), I will map out why this process should be viewed as a sacred journey, even as a pilgrimage, and convey the value for teens in casting the journey in this light. Herein, the college application process is presented, contrary to the way it is most often perceived by American teens, as a fecund opportunity to gain a deep understanding of themselves and their gifts to the world. I also explore why navigating the labyrinth (the symbolic enactment of ritual lostness that leads to a deeper understanding of the situation and the self) is such a powerful tool for centering, of rooting oneself and one's identity based on the inward work of one's own self-perception. Finally, I will also discuss why American youth so urgently need access to such tools.

The System Stressors

Although my clients' fear of the unknown and paralysis due to feelings of being overwhelmed by options and not in control of the outcome are counterproductive to the application process as journey toward self-discovery, those negative thoughts are utterly understandable. The cultural stressors that give rise to those feelings when wandering the college admissions landscape are many and powerful.

In an August 2013 study by Julie Vultaggio[1] and Stephen Friedfeld, college students were asked if their application process was stressful, and they were instructed to reflect on why that was the case if the answer was positive. One participant, who indicated the process was "incredibly stressful," stated, "[The process] was going to determine my entire future. I felt like making the slightest mistake would mean total failure." Another participant, who rated the process as "very stressful," described viewing college admission as "both the pinnacle of my life up until that point and as an integral part of my life and future." Obviously, this single decision is being viewed as happening in a vacuum of sorts, within a situation with parameters that are set in stone and the outcome of any single choice a given.

---

1 Vultaggio, Julie, and Friedfeld, Stephen. "Stressors in College Choice, Application and Decision-Making and How to Reduce Them" *Journal of College Admissions*, no. 211 (Fall 2013): 7.

Therefore, the decision is viewed as black or white: a singular right choice as opposed to multiple possible wrong ones.

Because I have witnessed gradually a marked increase in anxiety and other stress-related disorders among my clients surrounding applying to college, I have given much thought as to why they might feel more stressed than clients did some years ago. For one, there has been a marked increase in sophisticated marketing campaigns resulting in increased numbers of applications. This so-called "recruit to reject" strategy means the odds of rejection have gone up substantially. Thus this idea that there is a single right choice ups the ante substantially, but that is not the whole story behind the stress my young clients are displaying. The overemphasis on college admissions as the determiner of future success, which is inevitably accompanied by paranoia about mistakes and failures, originates from many sources. The stressors I have identified are certainly diverse.

- Parental fear of downward mobility: parents have grown increasingly concerned, which has perhaps been exacerbated by the Great Recession in the late 2000s, about the ability of their college graduate children to secure employment. Expectations regarding upward mobility are inherent to the American sense of self, and that mobility has a generational aspect based on economic history. Subsequent generations have tended to be better off economically than previous generations, but recent economic developments from mechanization to globalization have made this less a certainty.

- Family expectations in general: according to Vultaggio and Friedfeld, 57% of participants cited parents and family members as sources of stress in the college admissions process. Cultural messages regarding the importance of this step in life are not only held by the young undertaking this step, of course, but by all members of the culture, and especially parents, who are likely bankrolling the cost of this educational endeavor.

- Social media peer pressure: high schoolers today are far more aware of the activities of their peers than in past generations due to the popularity of social media. They have been comparing themselves to their peers constantly since they procured their first Smartphone, and I am constantly amazed at how many of them know where classmates have been admitted to college. The overall decision takes on aspects of a competition, wherein we metaphorically cheer for a select group that "wins" rather than a marathon wherein fans cheer on all of the participants simply because the endeavor has been valiantly attempted.

- Aggressive marketing by colleges: again, a practice that increases applications and consequently decreases acceptance rates, a metric utilized in rankings equations, which matter to colleges.

- Institutional priorities: the best-kept secret regarding admissions is that colleges have a vested interest in their positions in ranking hierarchies, from *US News & World Report* to the *Princeton Review*. So, not only do the odds go up with added applications achieved via the ranking system, but ranking itself is presented as an element in the decision and students are convinced they must get into a "good" school, an inflated conception based on manipulated acceptance rates.

- The rise in international student applicants: international students, who come from diverse backgrounds and perspectives and are frequently (if not exclusively) full-pay students with no need of financial aid, are appealing to selective American universities because their presence enables schools to discount tuition to attract stellar less-affluent students. As more and more applicants compete for fewer seats, institutional needs often trump admissions based on merit.

- Web-based resources are increasing the volume of applications: the Common Application (and other online applications in general, such as the Coalition for College Access), which can be completed once and then submitted to over 700 colleges, contributes to an increase in the number of college applications submitted—and why shouldn't a student apply to many, many schools if they don't have to complete separate applications for each? Consequently, if achieving a place at a given institution is viewed as a win and not achieving it perceived as a loss, then the odds against success have just gone way up.

- The increased use of data in the application process: the data used in rankings, in combination with web-based statistical tools that have proliferated as a means to construe outcomes, enables students to see how applicants match up with other students. Thus, when the process is viewed in black and white terms, as a win or lose proposition rather than a fit to be made among numerous viable options, students are prompted once again to focus outward on others as competition and not on the inner self. Naviance, for example, allows students to compare themselves to now-graduated schoolmates as points on a scatter diagram, GPA along one axis and test scores along the other—the points color-coded to show which students were accepted, waitlisted, or denied. In theory, the Naviance scattergram (and other software applications like Scoir, Niche and Guidedpath) apprises current applicants of their own odds based on the results of previous applicants. While these statistics have slightly increased the transparency of the metrics component of the process, they have also managed the expectations of students to the extent that some students won't even attempt to apply to schools that seem out of their league. However, the scatter diagram has limitations as a predictive tool. For example, it does not account for athletic recruiting, ethnic minority or diversity acceptances, legacy status, or development cases.

- En masse online release of admissions results: there is simply no opportunity for an applicant to sit quietly with his or her family and process the possible undesired outcome of rejection. One year, one of my clients did not attend school the day admissions decisions were released for a college because, although he claimed he wanted to be home and have access to a computer when the decisions were released, he ultimately admitted, "I just didn't want to face the public humiliation of not getting in while I was still struggling with my own emotions of disappointment."

- Lack of mechanisms to cope with stressors in healthy ways is an added stressor in and of itself. The three areas of primary wellness measurement (sleep, exercise, and diet) are under siege in our sedentary, screen-driven, fast-food-consuming culture; and an increase in anxiety and depression, and subsequently suicide rates as well, has occurred among American teenagers as a result. The decline of unstructured creative play throughout childhood might also be a contributor to the lack of such mechanisms as well as to stress itself. In lieu of encouraging play time, driven suburban parents (including, I must admit, myself) cart their children from skill-mastery activity to skill-mastery activity.

As noted by medical doctor and Brown University School of Medicine faculty member Esther Entin,

> By depriving children of opportunities to play on their own, away from the direct adult supervision and control, we are depriving them of opportunities to learn how to take control of their lives. We may think we are protecting them, but in fact we are diminishing their joy, diminishing their self-control, preventing them from discovering and exploring the endeavors they would most love, and increasing the chance that they will suffer from anxiety, depression, and various other mental disorders.[2]

In other words, not only are the young stressed by virtue of how they perceive the process because of how the culture formulates this choice for them in black and white terms, the "right" choice versus many possible wrong ones, but they have also often been deprived of instruction in coping mechanisms to manage the stresses, the process, and the outcomes of the college search in a healthy fashion.

• Tuition costs: the soaring cost of tuition has consistently outstripped inflation, doubling at many private colleges in only ten years. Consequently, graduates who took out student loans to finance their education are under a tremendous amount of strain from debt. With the investment so high, viewing the choice as black and white can mean viewing this strain as worth it or not as we will pursue below.

---

2   Entin, Esther, The Atlantic, https://www.theatlantic.com/health/archive/2011/10/all-work-and-no-play-why-your-kids-are-more-anxious-depressed/246422/

- Branding: colleges, like for-profit businesses, have achieved national name recognition through marketing tactics similar to America's most recognizable brands, like Nike and Jeep. The concept of exclusivity only seems to enhance the value of the brand. Research has shown that achievement pressure crosses all groups, even socioeconomics, so it is not just privileged teens that are bearing the burden of stress regarding getting into a school perceived to be on the list of "right" schools.

- The practice of over-rewarding children incessantly with accolades: millennials (a generation roughly defined as those born between 1980 and 2000) are sometimes labeled "the trophy generation" because they are always looking for the gold star, praise for their achievements.[3] This has resulted in a narcissistic generation who believe themselves entitled to be recognized as special. Students' sense of entitlement can be exacerbated at universities who value tuition dollars over the principle of exposing their students to a rigorous academic experience and thus treat their students as "customers to be pleased and placated."[4] Ironically, once in college, however, students' sense of entitlement can be supreme. So, if a student "wins" by being accepted to a given institution, their overall sense of self remains inflated and therefore distorted by the perception that they are superior to their rejected peers, and the culture continues down a path of hubris whereby the "ends justifying means" rather than producing fully formed adults who recognize that work ethic trumps name recognition post-college. Seeking recognition of one's self-esteem in the college process is a recipe for self-image

3   Pew Research Center, 2014.

4   Jeffrey Selingo, *College (Un)Bound: The Future of Higher Education and What it Means for Students* (New York: Houghton Mifflin Harcourt, 2013), xvii.

destruction. However, parents and students alike have begun to view the college process in light of that affirmation and to judge each other as a result of gaining access to the exclusive club of low-admit colleges.

Maintaining Mindfulness and Staying Centered in the College Admissions Process

Mindfulness, as used in this text, means being both aware of the college admissions process as it is defined by the culture and as it must be perceived contra that view if the applicant is to undertake this task in a healthy fashion. Mindfulness also includes self awareness, as in developing an understanding of self apart from the mirrors that culture and peers hold up to us, apart from internalized outside voices in favor of discovering and developing our authentic selves. The overall aim is not only to define the parameters of this process as regards the expectations of others but, more importantly, in terms of what is best for the student by keeping students centered, rooted in perceptions of self-worth and self-identity in order to emerge from this process a more fully formed adult prepared to embrace the often circuitous pathway of life and to withstand the "slings and arrows of outrageous fortune," to quote Shakespeare's "Hamlet," that are inevitably a part of any life.

The overall picture of the process of applying to college is thus painted for students as a zero-sum situation, and therefore a competition with others, and at mythic Hunger Games stakes, rather than students accepting the dynamic nature of being, itself, and of life in general and thus of the application process. Further, many are convinced that getting into the "right" college is a guarantee of personal, life-long net-worth. Students are not only subliminally encouraged to think of college application as a "golden ticket" but overtly as well by anomalous consultants who have failed to recognize that the emphasis of the process should be more on the student than on the schools. Many, perhaps ethically challenged, guidance professionals even overtly encourage students to "game" the system, regardless of the very high price of inauthenticity for the client, which they justify as necessary to attain the almighty goal of admission to a very selective institution.

That is, even without cheating or criminal conduct, as in Operation Varsity Blues, an outright scam that included many well-healed clients of a particular consultant, there are so-called "professional" college consultants who attempt to package students in order for them to appear as the ideal applicant to an institution. They advise the student to select strategically extracurricular activities that an institution might find attractive, even if the student is not passionate about, say, classical guitar, having given up cross country because he simply would not be good enough at this sport to be recruited. Such unethical practices call into question whether we, as a culture, are encouraging high schoolers to live authentic lives or create virtual ones by way of an application resume. Swiss developmental psychologist and philosopher Jean Piaget wrote extensively on the concept of *accommodation* (which he described as the act of trying to match oneself to something) versus *assimilation* (to become fully oneself without regard to the referent). By incorporating new experiences into one's schema, the basic set of values and behaviors that contribute to who a person is, only in order to become more fully "acceptable" to colleges' institutional priorities, students risk living lives of imitation. In fact, I would argue that remaining authentically who they are regardless of external stimuli rather than conforming to perceived formulae that have "worked" for other admitted students, students may in fact become even more attractive to admissions officers who are keenly aware of what a Temple University reader confided in me once called the difference between "wow" candidates and "imitation wow." If more students were exposed to the theory of assimilation, more might feel free to discover and decide who they are, declare what they are proud of among their accomplishments and activities, and then find those college cultures that match the student and not vice-versa. To do this, teens need encouragement, and they need authentic student-centered guidance. They need strategies and they need practice implementing those strategies. Rather than conforming, let alone appearing to conform, students seeking selective college admission should be striving actively to become the best version of themselves and no one else. As Oscar Wilde purportedly admonished, "Be yourself. Because everyone else is taken."

On that note, with all of the attributes of this perfect storm of the high-stakes college process, how can all caring, invested adults in a college applicant's life assist in diminishing disillusionment, anxiety and stress-related health issues, during the application process?

First, we can begin to shift the paradigm to encourage applicants to search for the *right* places and not necessarily the *best* places. What would constitute the right place in this redefinition of the term? One place to start might be in helping a student shift their focus to fit attributes that will help them grow and develop the skill set necessary to succeed beyond college. Rather than considering a career as an endpoint and their education as mere job training, we need to help them to appreciate higher education in the US as the opportunity to develop a transferable skill set that will amplify their value as a human. For example, what does studying to be an accountant, a theologian, or an engineer mean relative to who they are, who they wish to become, as a person as well as a professional?

Dispelling the myth of the *dream college* also helps students to break out of the crushing stranglehold of blind branding. For example, what difference will it make if they attend an institution with a high ranking if they will ultimately be straddled with three decades of debt or graduate in the lower portion of a larger, more competitive university, thereby compromising that student's ability to secure graduate school admission due to a lower GPA than she might have earned in a smaller institution. As stakeholders, we should simultaneously manage expectations and yet not crush dreams.

I do this in my practice by placing my students' GPA and test scores against the given college's admitted class metrics from the prior year. Then I ask them if it is a reach for them to apply to a particular school—in other words if they are likely to be admitted or if admission is in fact out of reach. I advise each student accordingly and help them sculpt a list of colleges where the best fit is balanced with reasonable expectations for choices once admissions decisions are made. However, changing the paradigm does not mean crushing dreams relative to that other paradigm of a black or white decision, but rather, we need to help students manage their expectations by helping them to craft a list that takes many attributes into consideration, including affordability if that is a concern for a given student and their family.

Happily, there are signs that some in higher education are recognizing the need for the college admissions paradigm to change. Initiatives that might attenuate the negative effects of applicant stress and that advocate for a more holistic approach for applicants are becoming apparent. For example, twenty percent of colleges in the United States do not require standardized test scores (namely the SAT or the ACT) to be considered for admission, and this number is steadily growing each year. This alone has opened opportunities for students who struggle mightily with test-taking anxiety. As of this writing, in addition, ACT has introduced the option to retake individual sections of the test which stands to benefit students, especially those who suffer with anxiety. Another prominent example is Harvard University's Graduate School of Education's "Turning the Tide II," a set of guidelines to help students develop their ethical character and maintain a less stressful environment when they are applying to colleges. This move shifts the emphasis from student value as metrics and test scores to a more accurate predictor—namely the four years of a student's classroom performance as evidenced in their transcript. Not only grades are considered but the rigor of the courses taken, which in turn allows applicants to consider, within the parameters of their high school and state's graduation requirements, what level of rigor will enable them to grow and remain amply challenged.

These are small steps on the part of higher education relative to the need to humanize this process, but they are nevertheless steps. However, the lack of institutional empathy and the tendency to view students as commodities and treat those they accept as "winners in life's race" at this stage in their lives risks attenuating the compassion with which they view anyone in society deemed lower in this arbitrary ranking hierarchy. The importance of empathy is amply apparent in my interaction with my clients. In fact, it is empathy and my attempt to humanize this process that teens routinely find most edifying (and sadly most absent in the system with which they are dealing). For example, I have spent the better part of an hour-long session listening to the frustrated catharsis of a rising senior whose GPA and activities are akin to that of a Rhodes Scholar but who suffers panic attacks in the reading comprehension section of the SAT, and she simply cannot increase her scores as a result. The system, in her view, does not care a whit about her issue in this regard in spite of her obvious talents.

Stakeholders can be vestiges of calm to such students, those struggling with the view of society that says they are not winners if they can't conform to a set of standards seemingly set in stone. Like Quasimodo in the film *The Hunchback of Notre Dame*, we can claim sanctuary and *be* sanctuary to teens during this liminal juncture by listening attentively, affirming movements toward the exploration of their most authentic selves, and dissipating any self-deprecation resulting from "not getting in." In doing so, we will wage a silent revolution over the current forces of the college search and admissions process that adversely impacts the emotional and psychological health of our youth.

What follows is my argument for the indispensability of including mindfulness as a weapon for self-defense against the societal pressures surrounding the college admissions process that are undermining the health and self-perception of our youth. The cost is simply too high in terms of a young person's sense of well-being. If we are to assist young people, we must be aware of these negative systemic forces and consciously denying their hold on a student's psyche. There is a very powerful tool to aid applicants in this regard, and we will now explore the possibility of incorporating that tool, the labyrinth, into our efforts to establish a mindful college search process. First, a cursory background of the labyrinth, conceptually and in practice through history, will show why this archetype is so effective with teens in the context of the college application process. Yet, first, we must further develop the nature and importance of the concept of liminality.

CHAPTER TWO

Nomads and Seekers of the Self

One of my former clients played Division I basketball at an Ivy League university and pursued a career as an investment banker after graduation. She revealed to me years later that she felt she could no longer proceed professionally with the lack of fulfillment she experienced in her life's work, and so she took an enormous drop in her income in favor of pursuing a more substantial experience than her career offered her, a year of voluntary service work in a small faith-sharing community. She observed, "The path to [investment banking] was so easy and enticing to enter, and yet so difficult to exit. My father can't understand why I would leave the security of, by his standards, a 'successful' career to pursue something more meaningful."

Defensiveness and fear are the predictable responses to discomfort when facing the unknown, even (and perhaps especially) for parents. While this example, under the operative paradigm for college choice, might seem to indicate the enormity of making the "right" choices from the beginning, this is merely proof of the new paradigm I am suggesting: life is a process rather than a product, and the expectations of others, and the values in this regard that we have internalized, do not vanish when we choose a college and a career. The point is that the process remains thus, a black or white, win/lose scenario filled with stress, unless and until, we reorient the approach to this process to include embracing the self-discovery and accept this as an opportunity to learn from mistakes and to grow as a human as a result.

Millennials are inherently very in tune with the variety of ways that they experience the world which is why they largely gravitate toward the "spiritual" versus "religion." In many ways, they are equipped with an internal GPS and are acquainted with the concept of the hero journey or quest from contemporary movies, literature and gaming. Sir Kenneth Robinson, an authority on education and the arts, argues that the entire objective of the American education system is to gain university admission, and students are convinced that they cannot afford to make mistakes on that path, which means squelching creativity in favor of conformity to a very narrow version of intelligence. By contrast, Robinson argues,

> If you're not prepared to be wrong, you'll never come up with anything original. We stigmatize mistakes. We are educating our children out of their creativity[5]... We need to radically rethink our view of intelligence... [I]t's diverse. We need to think about the world in all the ways that we experience it. We think visually. We think in sound. We think kinesthetically. We think in abstract terms. We think in movement."[6]

---

5   Ken Robinson, "How Schools Kill Creativity," accessed September 26, 2014, http://ted.com/talks/ken_robinson_says_schools_kill_creativity

6   Ibid.

The term *nomad*, invoking the idea of a lifestyle with no permanent ties to a community, is frequently used in theology to describe pilgrims wandering without a fixed home, and perhaps spiritually rather than as a physical fact. Arguably the most famous religious reference to a nomadic lifestyle is the Israelites wandering in the desert for forty years. I use the term to describe some students I researched and with whom I've worked in the context of educational consulting. Some of my clients seem more at ease with the unknowns of the process than others—especially those who have endured personal experiences of loss prompting a heightened familiarity with the unknown. I refer to them as nomads precisely because their orienteering skills in the face of the unknown that is the college process seems to have been heightened by their prior experiences with loss. "Many are in different stages of comfort on the journey... some are more comfortable than others with uncertainty."[7]

Allison (as with all clients mentioned herein, not her real name) was born with a severe spinal curvature and spent twenty-three hours per day in a back brace for most of her childhood. After several attempts at corrective surgeries, her spine continued to revert to its abnormal "S" shape. In her personal statement, she resisted discussing this adversity. "I don't see my spinal issues as interesting or unique in any way. It's just who I am and I don't want to call attention to it." Whether it's choosing not to go to the mall with friends, because she can't walk for long periods of time without rest, or not taking an advanced science lab because the lab's stools don't offer enough back support, Allison's condition does impact her everyday life. She embraces every type of difference she encounters. She has been known to wipe the faces of handicapped strangers who ask for assistance at a minor league baseball game. She also has a special

7   Ibid.

affinity for physically and mentally challenged children and peers; she volunteers with the Best Day Foundation, which organizes beach and snow play days for children with disabilities and their families and volunteers at a special needs residential summer camp annually.

Today, Allison is a registered nurse but even when I first met her, Allison was also shockingly at ease with the uncertainties of the college process, and in fact, she represents all of the attributes of a nomad in the college process: pliability, compassion, and the embrace of (versus recoiling from) not knowing. In 2019, Allison graduated with a Bachelor of Science in Nursing and has carved out a niche within the nursing field to allow her less time on her feet to attenuate the chronic back pain caused by her spinal condition. This is not to suggest that all students must be as at ease with the unknown as Allison, but rather, that the overall mindset for those embarking on this journey could be informed by her openness to outcomes, however unknown, and her obvious emphasis on the potentiality of the journey versus the arrival at an ultimate destination.

Launching into the Liminal

The term *liminal* is derived from a Latin word meaning "threshold," but in modern parlance has also come to mean the "space" a person inhabits during a transition. In folklore, the threshold plays an important role in the understanding of the familiar and the foreign. Ancient peoples believed that a god guarded the demarcations surrounding one's home, such as the Roman god, Janus, a two-faced god who looks in two directions: toward the occupants' home and toward the unknown. The further a traveler ventured away from the hearth, the more danger one risked encountering. In this instance, the threshold is the ground between what is safe, or home, and what is unknown, the wider world. In an age-old tradition of newlywed couples, the groom carries the bride over the threshold of their home, reflecting such ancient perceptions of transition, where the two become one and embark on a new adventure of shared life together. In a treatise on passage across thresholds, academic Johan Fornäs considers the significance of the creation of border experiences and touches on how various media can elicit this "in-between" stage of intellectual freedom, for that is what we are here defining this term to represent (as opposed to merely confusion or indecisiveness).

The threshold passages of liminal rituals are not limited to adolescence or sublime poetics alone. Practices of entertainment and popular culture as well as the various uses of communication media also induce several kinds of threshold states—between self and others, past and future, understanding and the unspeakable. Media play key roles in ritual processes that structure everyday life. The self-forgetful letting go in front of a novel, a sound system or a computer, opens experiential spaces where otherwise unconscious impulses may find expression through unexpected impressions. Such transitory experiences are better described in terms of thresholds for passages than as collisions with fixed borders.[8]

This explicit referral to "letting go" (as in, embarking on the twisting path from where one stands psychologically to where one is going) may be a critical step in the pursuit of one's center, arriving at insight, or coming into a state of contemplation.

In the famed stained glass of Chartres Cathedral in France, the Blessed Virgin Mary is found seated within an oval shape referred to as a *mandorla*, Italian for "almond." The shape is indeed that of an almond, roughly resembling the overlap of a Venn diagram.

---

8   Johan Fornäs, "Passages across Thresholds: Into the Borderlands of Mediation," Convergence: The Journal of Research into New Media Technologies (8) 4 (2002): 89-106, accessed July 26, 2014, http://diva-portal.org/smash/get/diva2:114229/FULL-TEXT01.info

Stained-glass artists use this symbolism to convey a state of transition, as from one world to the next, or to signify sacred moments that transcend time and space. It seems significant that there is a dedicated shape that signifies a transitional, in-between-worlds moment at which many artists have attempted to gesture throughout art history. Much like the Celtic spiritual concept of *thin places*, the *mandorla* is the opening that juxtaposes two worlds—the material and the spiritual. That is, any two states, whether material or spiritual/psychological, are connected by a period of liminality, of being both and neither at once, but this state is also the doorway between states, a necessary passage.

Transition inherently exposes both matter and human beings to uncertainty. Author Leonard Hjalmarson writes, "Liminality is a place in between. It is emptiness and nowhere. Adolescence is the liminal space between childhood and adulthood... Liminality is more than just a point along the way to somewhere else. It represents anti-structure to structure, chaos to order."[9] An applicant to college, with one foot in their old life but pondering a future they are struggling to envision, and under all the stressors listed previously on top of it all, is a prime example of liminality. The applicant is neither completed with their current stage in life nor can they claim the status of their imminent next step. They abide somewhere betwixt and between identities. The subjective feeling of this liminal status is akin to chaos, which we as stakeholders attempting to guide these young people must needs honor. This chaos can manifest in the applicant's behavior and mental state in numerous ways. Anyone who has experienced vertigo knows how disoriented and panicked an individual with this spontaneous condition can feel. Teens too may feel unanchored, not knowing how to constellate themselves,

9 Ibid., 1.

floating as if interstellarly. No wonder most want to get off of the ride as quickly as possible. Thus the title of one of Turner's books is indeed apt: *Betwixt and Between*.

It seems plausible, in light of Hjalmarson's assertion, that the reaction of college applicants to the state of chaos or disorder would play a significant role in their college application process. According to Karasek's demand/control model:

> ...the most adverse reactions of psychological strain occur...when the psychological demands of the job are high and the worker's decision latitude in the task is low. These undesirable stress-like reactions, which result when arousal is combined with restricted opportunities for action or coping with the stressor, are referred to as psychological strain.[10]

Traditional high school-aged applicants applying to highly selective institutions tend to feel that they have very little agency over the outcomes of their admission efforts. Combined with the other key factors increasing selectivity in college admissions discussed in the previous chapter—as well as the reported diminishment in sleep, exercise, and a clean, balanced diet of American teens—it is no wonder why stress and anxiety-related health risks are on the rise in this population of high-achieving teens.

Liminality is not only characteristically chaotic, however, but also accompanied by potential. Nothing new happens as long as we are inside of our self-constructed comfort zone. Liminality is where

---

10   Robert Karasek, "Demand/Control Model: A Social, Emotional, and Physiological Approach to Stress Risk and Active Behavior," *ILO Encyclopedia of Occupational Health and Safety* (2011), accessed July 1, 2014, http://diva-portal.org/smash/get/diva2:114229/FULLTEXT01.pdf

transformation happens. It is where we are, by definition, not in control of outcomes. Hjalmarson quotes Catholic writer-priest Richard Rohr, who states:

> Nothing good or creative emerges from business as usual. This is why much of the work of God is to get people into liminal space, and keep them there long enough so that they can learn something essential. It is the ultimate teachable space…maybe the only one.[11]

Although Rohr's assertion is within a Christian context, the overall concept can be viewed from any religious perspective and also a non-sectarian point of view. For example, I studied with Dr. Gilbert I. Bond while at Yale Divinity School, a phenomenologist who was preoccupied with the symbolism of the periphery, of the threshold, of liminality, and he used to ask us, "Where is the really exciting growth happening? In the well-organized and orderly field? Or is it on the wild edges?" Applicants to college are journeyers through liminal territory, standing in the doorway of their current life stage and looking outward into the wider world; and as such they constitute a nomadic tribe searching and eagerly awaiting their arrival on firm ground in their next life stage. We can now see why they struggle so with this abeyance of disorientation which can often mimic a sense of being lost.

Lost and Found

And indeed the chaos of liminality is akin to being lost; the panic and other distressing feelings are related because they prompt emotions associated with crisis. I can relate. When I was six years old, I became lost in a forest. My brother was playing Pop Warner football

---

11 Hjalmarson, 8.

at a local park, and I followed a family friend and his son to a nature trail. When they emerged from the forest, I was not with them and they did not know where I was. I proceeded deeper and deeper into the forest, getting more and more lost, before eventually stumbling into someone's backyard. The homeowner luckily drove me back to the football field and I was reunited with my family.

I had only been gone for over an hour, but I was so psychologically traumatized by this event that, whenever I revisit the experience in my memory, the same thing recurs in my mind's eye: I see a huge pile of leaves fall from the sky and block one of the paths before me (presumably the one leading me back to my parents). The fear of separation and being completely alone I experienced as a child was so horrific that I can still see the leaves falling as an adult.

As stakeholders primarily supporting adolescents throughout the college process, we often experience feelings as we strive to love and support the person in a liminal stage. Thus I share another parable of lostness, but this time as the adult witness. In a crowded theme park, my daughter, then five years old became separated from my husband Charlie and me. When I realized she was lost, panic suffused my utter being. Charlie and I screamed her name as we frantically searched the crowd. I fell to my knees on the ground as the possibility of never seeing her again crossed my mind. As the knowledge of a lost child began to circulate through the crowd, others joined in the search for her and another park guest actually prayed with me. Twenty long minutes later, white-blonde hair turned the corner. I took her up into my arms, tearfully praising and thanking God. My family and I have since returned to that park, and even to that very spot, but I remain very uneasy not only there but in all crowded places with my children.

The point in this second parable is not to reveal my epic parental fails, but rather, to elucidate that, whether parent or child, the feelings of panic, chaos, and fear are the same. They are essential parts of losing and loss in general. The trauma of being lost yielded changes within me: an encounter with a loss of boundaries, the stress of feeling out of control and having to make choices under duress. As the mother of the lost child, perhaps I felt even less in control than when I myself was lost. My daughter subsequently developed an attachment issue in the years that followed and was unable to attend sleepovers and suffered mightily at brief sleep-away camp experiences. I enabled that fearful behavior for years, even though I knew it was limiting her from living her life to the fullest. However, ultimately I acknowledged the traumatic impact of that experience at such a tender age and reviewed my own behaviors around trying to protect and rescue her from her fears. I realized this was counterproductive, and we then began to talk about and process our mutual experience of lostness and tried to draw connections. This process ultimately gave her permission to recognize the emotions her lostness evoked and how to develop tools for her to cope and move through them.

This is an example of how liminality is where transformation happens. Metaphorically speaking, sometimes one must lose herself to find herself. The chaos of liminality is tantamount to being lost in as much as one's identity is in flux, one's sense of self betwixt and between life stages. The fact is that one cannot find one's new self without the old version of self being lost in the process, and that feeling of lostness is truly disconcerting. Indeed, this feeling of being lost while on the way to being found, to finding one's new sense of self, is the context within which I work as I help my clients through the process of exploring options for their continuing education.

Tully, a client of my educational consulting practice, was six years old when his father was killed in the terrorist attacks of September 11, 2001. He had found significant academic success, especially in science, and in football. In our first sessions, he was taciturn, respectful but reticent, sharing little except one-word replies. The violent loss of a parent had a profound and traumatic impact on him. It was at the end of our third meeting that I asked if he had any film of his football games to share with colleges. He, in fact, had a highlight video on YouTube of footage from his junior year season. It was remarkable, and my jaw dropped as I observed his explosive prowess, play after play.

In an essay-brainstorming activity during the following session, Tully shared with me his disappointment over not having his father present, especially to help him with football. "My father had played Division I football," he told me, "and many of my teammates' fathers are very active in their athletic development." Tully was clearly grieving that loss of companionship, and he expressed that sorrow in our conversations as a what-might-have-been. This sense of loss was particularly poignant for him as he prepared to leave the familiarity of home and transition into a new and precarious stage of his life, that of emerging adulthood. Tully, through much teasing out, shared intimate stories of how he keeps his father's memory close by stitching his father's initials inside his football cleats. He wrote a beautiful essay about his loss and how football has been a vehicle to maintain a close tie to his departed father. In his self-exploration, because he had navigated the traumatic loss of a parent, Tully was more at ease with the feelings of disorientation as opposed to other students who have not encountered such a loss. It appeared that he achieved a step toward a new identity by virtue of his journey through loss, that he had emerged from that terrible experience with the special gift of being accustomed to the unknown and, thereby, was not as intimidated by the feelings that often accompany that step.

I have observed that the more time a student spends learning about themselves the more the student disengages from competing with their peers, a stressor mentioned previously, the tendency to compare and look outward rather than dedicate time to personal self-reflection. Those who are not preoccupied with constant comparison with peers focus more on the task at hand: establishing the best-fit college or learning environment for themselves. In a sense, the more a person explores their self conception relative to impending changes in life the less they feel lost while navigating these unfamiliar waters. Thus, there is a feedback loop-like correlation between lostness and self-discovery in liminality that allows a person to feel more at home in this liminal landscape precisely because they are discovering things about themselves that make this journey less disconcerting. During this time of liminal lost-ness, many of these students are finding out who they really are.

Tully seems much more at ease in the unknowns of the college process and outcomes than the "typical" candidate. He did not manifest a sense of fear or notable anxiety. It appeared that he felt at ease in this cloud of unknowing, with the feeling of being lost, because it had been the normative orientation throughout his young life. With that sense of lostness had come other heightened senses, like his inordinately strong sense of social justice, fierce loyalty, and honesty. Because a sense of liminality had been part of his sense of himself since he had lost his father, he was better equipped than most to embark on the college process, one fraught with unknowns by definition, but he also willingly explored who he was relative to losing a loved one and to the process of applying to college. It was this growth that was a result of his familiarity with lostness that allowed him to accept an early decision rejection and a subsequent Ivy League acceptance. In fact, Tully's was one of the most adventurous journeys I have witnessed in my decades of doing this work. When I saw him on the field in his orange and black football uniform, I was delighted to witness his firm sense of self, continuing to do what he loved at the college level.

I have been personally touched by the loss of a dozen friends and acquaintances on 9/11, and every year for the first decade of my practice, I had the opportunity to work with applicants who lost parents and siblings that day. Any transition, but especially the transition from high school to college, has the potential to reawaken unresolved feelings of remorse and disorientation. As such, I was pleased to provide professional guidance throughout this season of uncertainty to numerous families who suffered the loss of a family member on 9/11.

For example, one of my clients, after a few brainstorming exercises to help her explore college essay topics, began to sob uncontrollably. Shanley had lost her father on 9/11, and she described how she had never fully grieved this loss and how visual art became her means of self-expression. According to her:

> It [art] literally saved my life… I was so young when it
> all happened. My two older sisters were at least mobile,
> had friends and access to cars. My grief and I were
> confined to my house. When I entered high school, an
> art teacher exposed me to the world of self-expression
> through painting, drawing, creativity.[12]

---

12 Erin Avery, Healing Hope: Spiritual Encounters of 9/11's Loved Ones (self-published, 2012), 7.

Through the medium of art, Shanley was able to process the painful feelings of loss surrounding her father's death, and writing about it in her college essay granted her permission to continue moving through the stages of grief and loss. She and I collaborated to create a commemoration for the eleventh anniversary of the attacks, incorporating her emotionally-cathartic paintings along with stories I collected from loved ones who lost family members and felt profound connections to them after their deaths. We self-published a small literary magazine called *Healing Hope*. This is just one example of how adult stakeholders can assist students in the act of creating sanctuary when transition triggers unresolved vulnerabilities in our beloved young people.

In fact, the journey through liminal territory is not merely an opportunity for self-discovery, and an especially fecund opportunity for those who have suffered loss, but it allows those young people an overt reason to revisit the loss through the self-discovery inherent in the college application process should they choose to write about it in their personal statement. Shanley's vehicle of working through the stages of grief was art, and Tully's was through competing at football. The responsibility of stakeholders privileged to journey alongside teens in this process is profound, and the potential possibilities for growth and healing are equally profound. To overlook the potentiality in this process is to squander a prime opportunity to foster healing and restore a semblance of wholeness to any young person who has experienced loss. In expressing her unresolved grief, Shanley was able to connect with adults in her life and move through the painful loss productively. An adult joining her in her journey proved to be a powerful means of her feeling less lost in the college process. She was ultimately accepted to a premier visual arts program, and her strengths have now helped her audiences to recognize the power of personal reflection in the midst of liminality.

A Season of Uncertainty

However, the obstacle that the current college admissions paradigm presents, that of furtiveness and competition, is enormous and not easily overcome. I once had a client who was so desperate to fast-forward through the college process so as to skip the stress and discomfort of uncertainty that, in our first session, she blurted out, "I just want it over with. I just want the sticker on the back of my car!" One might be tempted to chalk this up to a typical immediate gratification response. However, I have come to understand that it is fueled more by the desire to return to the comfort of order and what to expect next.

In my educational consulting practice, it has been my increasing desire to revere and validate this space of unknowing, this liminal time between one firm sense of one's place/role in the world and the next firm sense of the same, as a time of as a time of great potential. I've always bemoaned the glossing over of the momentous gravity of the "now" in favor of reestablishing security as quickly as possible. If Shanley had sped through the application process, for example, she might have missed the profound opportunity to confront many unresolved questions and concerns regarding the traumatic loss of her father. As Hjalmarson so insightfully writes, "This is the benefit of liminality… We let go of the old answers and begin to ask new ones."[13]

This process, the journey through liminality, enables agency, or one's own ability to choose and act. That is, you have a choice regarding whether you remain in a settled place or choose a journey.

---

13 Hjalmarson, 4.

If you choose to embrace the journey, the possibilities—the twists and turns of the unknown—will seem like an adventure. If you cleave to the known, anything unknown will remain stressful, even fear-inducing. Truly to embrace the inherent nature of the college search and application process, we must first choose to shift the paradigm from fearful apprehension to adventurous embrace.

Anthropologists Victor and Edith Turner draw a distinction between liminal and liminoid, the former a journey one undertakes because they *have to* and the latter an experience that has liminal characteristics but that one *chooses* to undertake. Since pilgrimage is voluntary and not an obligation, "...pilgrimage is best thought out as 'liminoid' or 'quasi-liminal' rather than 'liminal.'"[14] I frequently ponder whether high-achieving high school students feel that attending college is a choice rather than an obligation. Are they being thrust into the process? Does their process reflect a true liminal experience, such as adolescence, or have they paused to consciously consider and choose the path before them?

In my intake of new students, I always ask them, "Do you want to go to college?" I almost always receive an affirmative answer, but I wonder how much teens are influenced by the messages of contemporary culture, wherein college is marketed as a social experience or rite of passage rather than an intellectual continuation of study. By asking my students if they want to attend college, I mean to ask them if they are choosing to continue their studies or choosing to protract their adolescent liminality (with an added weighty price tag). In other words, is the student making a conscious, as opposed to an involuntary, choice to begin the pursuit of higher education?

In the May 9, 2011 issue of *New York Magazine*, the cover teaser of an article reads, "Is College a Scam?" The article itself is entitled

14 Turner and Turner, 35.

"The University Has No Clothes," and in it, two graduates of prestigious schools, Stanford and Cornell respectively, observe: "[It's] hard to think of a time when the skepticism of the value of higher education has been more prominent than it is right now."[15]

"The cost of education in the past thirty years has gone up six-fold and inflation has only gone up threefold," according to James Altucher, a New York-based venture capitalist and finance writer. Even PayPal co-founder Peter Thiel feels that a bubble in college tuition may be coming based on the signs: "hyperinflated prices, investments by ignorant consumers funded largely by debt and widespread faith in increasing returns." Thiel is the founder of 20 Under 20, an initiative that grants twenty individuals aged nineteen or over $100,000 for entrepreneurial ventures. The catch? They cannot enroll in college for at least two years.[16]

What's more, student loan debt in the United States exceeds a trillion dollars. It's no wonder, then, why parents and families are asking about the return on investment. The *New York Magazine* article posits that colleges have become "corporate-minded youth resorts" versus rigorous intellectual communities. This article, and others in the *Chronicle of Higher Education* and the *Atlantic*, at the very least have prompted curiosity regarding the indispensability of college. Perhaps more exposure to these questions will assist applicants in making the journey a liminoid, instead of a liminal, rite of passage by voluntarily undertaking the journey. It is valid then to question the old paradigm that suggests that financial security is tied to a college degree. Is the return on this investment disappearing as young people who finance their education with loans are being saddled with debt that may take their entire working lives or beyond to pay

---

15   Daniel Smith, "The University Has No Clothes," *New York Magazine* (May 9, 2011): 44.
16   Ibid, 44.

off? I encountered a staggering statistic noting the number of retirees last year whose Social Security checks were being garnished due to unpaid student loans!

I courageously raise the specter of not even getting out of the old paradigm what it seemed to promise because I believe, as do many of my professional colleagues, that we may be closer to the bubble bursting than many think. The topic is beyond the scope of this writing, but by casting the college question as a sacred journey we begin not only to validate the personhood of the applicant but also to contemplate whether college at the moment is indeed the proper next step for each and every individual applicant. And the best way to step away from the "group think" that attending college fulltime in the traditional time frame of ages 18-22 is to encourage young people to pause and reflect, both on what the culture at large is telling them about college that may not be true and on their own needs and goals relative to who they are. In a word, raising this issue is a necessary part of the mindfulness necessary in the process as journey.

Isolation in the Process: Shifting the College Paradigm in Search of Communitas

In my work, I have witnessed several trends in student behavior that reflect the isolation and alienation that adolescents experience in the process. The Turners observe, "Friendship and community are critical pieces in the journey forward. In order to embrace the new, we have to grieve the loss of the old. Few of us are capable of doing that work alone: healthily processing grief requires community and friendship."[17] But high school students do make this journey alone, and in some circles they are advised not even to speak to each other about the colleges to which they're applying so as to

17 Hjalmarson, 7.

conceal their choices from other potential competition. The public nature of social media has amplified this—competitive comparisons of varying opportunities (and students' subsequent resentment of their peers) are commonplace. For example, when a student in my research was accepted to Cornell, two of his peers snidely oversimplified his success by saying, "Yeah, just teach lacrosse to little kids and you, too, can get into an Ivy League." In one sense, although dismissive and cynical, they nevertheless seem to have grasped the overall cynicism of a process based on lists of accomplishments/activities that are presumed to represent who a person is.

As a result of such potential reactions by peers and because of the advice in some quarters noted above, the college process is an arena where some students deliberately attempt to conceal their actions as a competitive tactic to attempt to increase one's position and decrease competition but also to hide both their perceived successes and their failures so as not to awaken snarky commentators. In fact, students grow so paranoid that their peers become merely competitors rather than members of the community to which they, in fact, all belong: journeyers on like paths.

In Victor and Edith Turner's seminal book, *Image and Pilgrimage in Christian Culture*, the authors explore the notion of the rite of passage. While they do this in the context of religious pilgrimages, they give much thought to the notion of liminality. In the liminal state of embarking on a pilgrimage, which is in fact a rite of passage whereby the journeyer is moving not only from a given place to another physically but spiritually as well, the Turners recognize much possibility. "It has become clear to us that liminality is not only transition but also potentiality, not only 'going to be' but also 'what may be...'"[18] And because pilgrimage is completely volitional, "...

---

18   Turner and Turner, 3.

pilgrimage may be said to represent the quintessence of voluntary liminality."[19] In other words, the journey undertaken as a matter of choice becomes the ground of maximum choice as regards change. That is, liminality, according to the Turners, is a state of individual consciousness, of personal searching, but that does not mean one is alone in their search. The Turners coined a term for the experience of losing one's old identity and freely and spontaneously encountering others on the pilgrimage to a new identity: *communitas*. A sense of *communitas* allows for solidarity and is a profound opportunity for deep friendship. As in any rite of passage, the person hopes to return from their pilgrimage renewed, even transformed, and if they find communitas, they have help along the way from, and provide help to, others seeking a similar renewal and transformation.[20] Anyone who has become fast friends on a vacation or at camp comprehends this phenomenon.

As part of my practice I offer an annual "College Application Boot Camp." In the twelve years I have offered this camp, I have noticed the enjoyment that this small group of eight to 12 students experiences in completing the process of their online Common Application together. One student observed, "It's really motivating to do this together. I would really have a hard time doing this alone, sitting at home by myself." Another said, "By adding pizza and a mid-session break, we got to be kids again and not just application robots."

Many of these students add one another as friends on social media and stay in touch after this intense experience of eight hours over one week together. As humans, we resist discomfort or

19   Ibid., 9.

20   Simon Coleman, "Pilgrims and Pilgrimage: Social Anthropology," accessed June 1, 2014, http://www.york.ac.uk/projects/pilgrimage/content/soc_anth.html

vulnerability and why wouldn't we? "Anxiety pushes us into conditioned responses (fight or flight); yet safety allows us to move forward and explore the unknown with open hands and open hearts."[21] The communal aspect of the annual boot camp dissipates some of these feelings of vulnerability, and as the individuals in the group recognize that they are not alone, they begin to come together as a community.

The sense of being lost on this journey toward college, if shared and affirmed with other sojourners, can open up opportunities for peer leadership and mentorship, and the solidarity these students achieve can help to reduce the overall stress of the process.

A Pilgrim's Progress

When one embarks on a traditional spiritual pilgrimage, certain premises remain and have held through history. The pilgrimage is often considered a microcosm of the earthly journey, an allotted period of time during which the traveler sets out on a quest; and along the way, the pilgrim, in their vulnerability, relies on both the hospitality and generosity of others to complete the quest. The desired outcome of the journey is the hope of a greater awareness of self and of a higher power, and the prerequisite is vulnerability or perhaps humility.

I have noted some connections and overlaps between the college search and a pilgrimage from my own experiences:

- Both require leaving behind the comfort of the familiar.

- Both require the participant to seek deeper self-understanding.

- Both bear the promise of a destination.

---

21 Hjalmarson, 8.

- Both include the hallmarks of initiation: separation, liminality, and reintegration.

- Both demand intention.

- Both required openness to surprising encounters that lay beyond the control of the journeyer to imagine or plan.

Chinese philosopher Lao Tse once wrote, "The journey of a thousand miles begins with one step." The journey's first step is in fact an examination of the interior self, and that examination is the lens through which I encourage my students to view their college process. That is, this lens is not like a telescope that allows us to look outward but a lens we turn inward to look deeply into ourselves. In looking inward, we begin the life-long journey of self-understanding. We do not all think alike or learn alike. In fact, genius can manifest quite differently in two individuals.

Whereas the old paradigm tends to assume that the orientation of any single person to the world is the same, Howard Gardner's theory of multiple intelligences suggests otherwise. Moreover, any person's understanding of the world is not merely a function of abstract reason, but of their varied strengths.

I first noticed this distinction when, at a young age, I pondered why I so nonchalantly navigated the rigors of traditional classroom education while one of my sisters struggled so mightily with it. Eight years my junior, Julia went on to play Division I field hockey at the University of Virginia, and she set countless scoring records during her high school career, but learning was a self-professed chore for her.

Julia, I believe, is a textbook kinesthetic learner. Kinesthetic learning is a subset of active learning that includes physical activity. When kinesthetic principles are recognized, activity is used "...in the classroom with the objective of introducing and strengthening concepts as well as connecting ideas together." However, the amount of instances in which teachers use this type of engaged learning "… drops to nearly zero as students progress from primary to secondary to post-secondary school."[22] However, some people learn predominantly via their physical association with the world, and so, this drop off in such classroom strategies explains why learning becomes an increasing struggle for students who learn predominantly kinesthetically. However, we all have access to the various learning styles, and indeed, learning by physically doing, albeit discounted in education as students reach the higher grades, remains one of our primary means to gain new skills. Educators from Maria Montessori to Jean Piaget to Charlotte Mason have emphasized that the first means of discovering the world is through the physical, and it remains a means by which to learn throughout our lives:

As the brain matures, facts are abstracted and related to other concepts. Although the ability to abstract a concept and make complex connections between concepts are considered to be signatures of a mature mind, humans learn best by doing something concrete first, and then abstracting to more general concepts.[23]

This notion of "doing something concrete first" is what walking the labyrinth can amount to for students applying to college, and from my own experiences, when done at the outset of the college search, the experience creates a physical metaphor that sets the framework for understanding and speaking about what is happening throughout the college application process.

Proprioception pertains to stimuli that are produced and perceived within an organism, especially those connected with the

22   "Kinesthetic Learning in the Classroom," accessed August 16, 2014, http://www.facstaff.bucknell.edu/jvt002/Docs/ASEE-2008b.pdf, 1.

23   Ibid.

position and movement of the body. It refers to a spatial awareness of the relative position of neighboring parts of the body and strength of effort being employed in movement. Being an elite athlete, my sister, Julia, could be classified as having a Mensa-level mastery of proprioception. Yet, sit her in a lecture-style class and she might promptly lose focus and motivation. In moving, she was connecting to her source of greatest knowledge. However, all of us, no matter our capacity for abstract reason, have the same proprioceptive basis for our relationship to the world, and it is upon this "knowledge" that we can leverage the labyrinth experience to access experiential learning about ourselves.

In addition to working with high schoolers applying to college, I work with middle schoolers applying to independent boarding schools. Being that my work with this demographic was within one geographic area for many years, I kept encountering the same response to a stock essay prompt on the Secondary School Admissions Testing Board application: "Who is your favorite teacher and why?" I became acquainted with Mr. Garside, who taught seventh- and eighth-grade science at Rumson Country Day School. As I probed students regarding their affection for this teacher, it became clear to me that he regularly incorporated kinesthetic learning in his classes:

"In Mr. Garside's class, we made garbage bags levitate on the football field!"

"He has something called 'Burn Everything Day' when we light the Bunsen burners and take turns setting different substances on fire!"

"Every spring, Mr. Garside takes us to Physics Day at Six Flags and we get to go on rides and hold instruments and measure things like the velocity of a roller coaster!"

While some students might be tempted to treat these activities as mental recess, Mr. Garside had so thoroughly mastered how to link an activity with a concept and follow with debriefing to bind tightly the experience with mastery of the concept at hand that students could not help but learn from and love these exercises. We the adults and educators/counselors can assist teens to consider new ways of learning and leaning into the college process that validate their humanity and variety of learning styles.

Based on the concepts discussed in this chapter, I am proposing that we shift the paradigm of the college application process from a black/white, right/wrong decision based on what the culture at large tells students they should aspire to in favor of a dynamic process of self-realization. I am suggesting we view the college process as a pilgrimage, a quasi-sacred journey in and of itself in as much as the goal is one of transformation, of moving through the territory of lostness to achieve a new notion of self, and I am suggesting that we incorporate a kinesthetic learning activity to assist students in parsing how the process will work for them. The framework of the labyrinth is just such a physical activity. Thus, the new paradigm I am suggesting, the application process as a journey within which students can reflect and explore rather than merely engaging in a win/lose task is then projected outward from abstract processing to become an actual journey in the form of the labyrinth. Walking the physical labyrinth is not merely a metaphor for the journey of life but a kinesthetic learning activity that allows students to mindfully reflect in the format of a moving meditation. The experience thereby assists them in attenuating the outside cacophony, and subsequently, helps them grow in self-knowledge and understanding, helps them to root themselves in their life's purpose and establish whether higher education plays a role in that purpose and what institutions are the best fit for the person they have realized they are and desire to become.

CHAPTER THREE

The Labyrinth as Laboratory

Prospective students embarking on the college search and application process have many questions, mostly pertaining to the process itself: what tests should I take, what courses are required, what will I write about in my personal statement? There are, however, other pertinent questions that are equally vital for students to ask. Do I have any passions? At what do I excel? What makes me unique? Ultimately, what is my story? There exist myriad other pertinent questions, even if the old paradigm remains in play, let alone if students grasp the process as a journey, that are equally vital to striving toward the goal of a purposeful life.

Reflection is necessary to address these and other questions— and reflection, like any deep work, involves silence, space, and time. If you were to ask a typical teenager how often they enjoy silence during their day, you will discover what I have in my research and in my own experience: frequently never. Many of the boarding school students with whom I've worked and those I have studied are not alone for even a moment of the day! Lacking virtually any time for silent reflection, when are students expected to pursue the bigger questions such as their life's purpose?

A majority of millennials, when polled, self-report as "seekers" with intense spiritual yearning.[24] But the busier young people become, the more distracted they can be from pursuing those deeper questions that require separation from the constant din of the quotidian. They noticeably lack an experience of centeredness, of maintaining and nourishing a sense of inner peace that is required of anyone hoping to acquaint themselves with the deep mystery that is the self.

Viewing the college application process as a journey offers a profound opportunity for applicants to utilize this transitional period to help them achieve reflection, centering, and discernment, and a greater focus on student centeredness in the process can be achieved by investigating the archetype of the labyrinth. In my experience, many high school students' true feelings and perceptions regarding the college search process are negative, and they would benefit greatly from learning about a meditative archetype that will help them maintain a sense of sanity as they complete the journey.

As we have established, liminality is a sense of lostness, of chaos even, and as such, applicants want to re-achieve some semblance of peace represented by having achieved the next step (college), which, because of the paradigm under which they are conducting their search, they think is a do-or-die proposition. Liminality then is a space within which to explore self and world, a lab where students can perform thought experiments regarding their future, a place of experimentation where silence can be achieved and movement can be incorporated into the search of self. The ultimate goal of walking the labyrinth is to purge oneself of all external expectations while silently walking and meditating on the self, to become

24   David Kinnaman, *You Lost Me: Why Young Christians are Leaving Church…and Rethinking Faith* (Grand Rapids: Baker Books, 2011), 59.

more deliberate about the choices ahead and more aware of each individual applicant's unique giftedness.

The Walking Labyrinth

The labyrinth as a tool for self-discovery in navigating major life changes has been used in modern times in both spiritual and non-sectarian settings for the purpose of increasing health and self-awareness. Marked by a unicursal path, the walking labyrinth literally begins where it ends—the path in and the path out are identical. Unlike a maze, which is full of twists and turns and dead ends, labyrinths do not impede a walker with obstacles and force them to turn back.[25] Some scholars believe that the labyrinth walk is part of seven movements in ritual transformation (such as Geoffrion's stages: preparation, invocation, going in, staying at the center, returning, thanksgiving, and reflection).[26] And much of the material written about labyrinths describes three distinct movements that comprise the experience within the labyrinth: moving toward the center, arriving at the center, and the return trip.[27] That is, this symbolic journey can be used as a personal ritual within this separate space where the walker can detach from the material world and effectively purge stress-inducing triggers, for example in the first movement of the labyrinth walk: moving toward the center. Arriving at the center, the second stage, is symbolically arriving at centeredness, the psychological place where a walker is free to welcome, receive, or ponder a new awareness of self within the clarity provided by the purgation of the external distractors or definitions of self. And the return trip,

---

25 "Maze versus Labyrinth," accessed October 21, 2014, http://www.veriditas.org/Resources/Pictures/Labyrinth_vs_maze.png.

26 "Praying the Labyrinth," accessed October 1, 2014, http://jillgeoffrion.com/Labyrinth/Prayer/labyrinth7step.html

27 Arnold Van Geneep, *The Rites of Passage* (Chicago: University of Chicago Press, 1960), 57-62.

the third stage, is then symbolic of rejoining the community with increased self-awareness and a calm and centered disposition. "Yes, please!" say all parents of teens in unison.

Labyrinths are also used in religious and spiritual practices as an aid to meditation and spiritual awakening. A flier available for walkers of the labyrinth at the Woodlawn Cemetery in Florida refers to the three stages of the walk this way: purgation, illumination, and union. Purgation signifies the shedding or letting go that occurs as one begins the first phase of the labyrinth walk. Next, the walker may experience illumination through prayer or reflection when lingering at the center of the labyrinth. Finally, the walker may experience union with a higher power as they consider what they have encountered or learned while quieting the mind in this moving form of meditation. The threefold movement mimics the stages of rites of passage as delineated by Deborah Ross and the Turners:

> During a rite of passage a person enters a phase of separation from a previous group, which is followed by an in-between, or liminal, phase during which many aspects of life are likely to go through a process of change or distortion. Finally, there is a phase of reintegration into the community and entrance into a new social state.[28]

The labyrinth as symbol of the journey of life has achieved the level of archetype in modern usage, and in both spiritual and secular settings, and the psychological stages have been much discussed and elaborated upon; but the symbol system itself has a long

---

28   Victor Turner and Edith Turner, *Image and Pilgrimage in Christian Culture* (New York: Columbia University Press, 2011).

history that indicates the long-held efficacy of the labyrinth as tool for the sacred journey and the transformation of the self.

The Labyrinth and the Proliferation of an Archetype

The earliest recorded mention of the term labyrinth is found in records from ancient Egypt and is a reference to a structure erected in honor of twelve rulers. This massive structure, detailed by such historians as Pliny, consisted of elaborate rooms both above and below ground, such that one might get lost meandering through it. It was said to have exceeded even the pyramids in its grandiosity![29]

The most prominent mention of the labyrinth comes from Greek mythology. Constructed by Daedalus at the behest of King Minos, the labyrinth was located in Knossos on the island of Crete. Built underneath the royal palace and intended as a dwelling for the Minotaur, a half-human and half-bull creature born of the queen, who had been impregnated by a white bull as a result of the gods' trickery. Perhaps out of shame, the king banished this child to the depths of his palace. Due to a political rub between Crete and Athens, seven young Athenian men and women were sent annually to Knossos to face the Minotaur. None ever returned. Eventually, Theseus, the son of King Aegeus of Athens, offered himself as tribute in a valiant attempt to slay the Minotaur. He receives assistance from Ariadne, the daughter of King Minos (and incidentally the half-sister of the Minotaur), in the form of a clew (or spool) of thread to fasten to the entrance to the labyrinth and help him find his way back. Theseus, using the thread, winds his way to the center of the labyrinth, slays the Minotaur, and navigates his way to the exit. Indeed, I have often pondered whether we as stakeholders in

---

29 W.H. Matthews, *Mazes and Labyrinths: A General Account of their History and Development* (New York: Longmans, Green, and Co., 1922), 12-16.

students' academic journeys might view ourselves as the clew, helping the hero to identify his or her own path to the journey's completion.

Labyrinths begin to surface throughout the continents in various indigenous communities as disparate as India and North America. Maritime fishing communities assemble them out of stones. They are carved in rock in England. Some communities even assembled them out of peat.

The medieval labyrinth was developed during the ninth and tenth centuries CE and is commonly found in medieval churches and cathedrals in Europe. The most famous example is on the floor of Chartres Cathedral in France where it was inlaid into the floors during the cathedral's construction in the twelfth century. Differing from the classical style of seven circuits, it is an eleven-circuit labyrinth (the eleven concentric rings of paths that surround the center are known as circuits).[30]

Scholars and architects have long debated the precise use of the labyrinths in cathedrals simply because there are few existing sources describing its use. Some have suggested the labyrinth was a form of prayerful vicarious pilgrimage during the Crusades. It is also conjectured that there were other ancient rituals associated with labyrinth walking now lost due to the lack of written records.

> It was a path of initiation, a path of pilgrimage. In the
> early Gothic Easter rituals it was used as a dancing
> ground much as the classical labyrinth was used almost
> three thousand years ago. For three hundred years, this

---

30 Gael D. Hancock, *108 Ways to Use Labyrinths in Schools* (Las Vegas: Hancock & Associates, 2007), 7.

Easter dance was a customary component of the annual liturgy. Then it disappeared.[31]

It is hard to imagine at this post-Enlightenment, postmodern juncture that, on the evening of Easter Sunday, priests danced the length of the labyrinth, possibly symbolizing Christ's decent into Hell and triumphant victory over death. But how else might this peripatetic pattern have been used? We have some legal documentation that reveals that a labyrinth ritual involved a ball, possibly representing a sphere. The documentation involves a disgruntled young clergy member who felt he was unfairly assigned the financial responsibility for purchasing the yellow sphere or ball. Nonetheless, the labyrinth's possible Christian association with the symbolic death and rebirth narrative connects with the conceptions of being lost and being found, of the liminal space of abiding between death and life while awaiting the third day.

The labyrinth has many modern uses, some drawing from interpretations of religious uses of long ago that are recognized as having a psychological transformation correlative for the person taking the journey.

A Pause for Reflection

My initial encounter with a walking labyrinth revealed my lack of proper preparation and intentionality. I distinctly recall setting foot in the labyrinth, a donated monument dedicated to the memory of my father's college roommate nearly a decade ago, at the Upper Room Spiritual Center in Neptune, New Jersey. I have always been curious about the labyrinth's pattern, and I wanted to see what all the fuss was about it. I promptly abandoned the seemingly foolish

---

31   Candolini, Gernot, Labyrinths: Walking Toward the Center (New York: Crossroads, 2001), 93.

endeavor and walked away, dismissing the activity as a waste of time. I remember feeling uncomfortable with the redundancy and apparent pointlessness of the sinuous twists and turns. I walked out across the prescribed paths and hopped in my car, half-heartedly committing to return one day when I had less pressing matters to address.

After many years of consulting, of trying to figure out how to help my clients achieve better outcomes while attenuating the ever-increasing stress they confided they felt, it occurred to me that students needed a method of ritual transformation to get off of their phones, to get quiet, but they also needed to move, and ideally be out of doors while doing so. They needed to carve out space to accomplish these objectives, getting quiet and moving, and so did I. I traveled to a labyrinth in Gotha, Florida, and this time, I was prepared. I had traveled miles on a plane and had set aside time and space away from my family and the everyday frenetic pace of my own life to quiet down and embark on a somewhat mysterious journey. I now see that carving out that time for quiet exploration amounted to establishing a sacred space and was a critical affirmation of what I believe is a necessary investment in one's wellness.

Now it seems impossible that I could have ever deemed walking a labyrinth to be a ridiculous waste of time. I now know what deep and meaningful epiphanies are available from carving out time to ponder and reflect. I have since walked labyrinths throughout the country and world in the context of my research, as I was writing my doctoral dissertation, and as I have implemented lessons I've learned in guiding my clients through the college process.

I am, however, not alone in using the labyrinth archetype with students and young people. One of the many resources for this purpose is *108 Ways to Use Labyrinths in Schools* by Gael D. Hancock. Other individuals and organizations, such as Dr. Lauren Artress and the organization Veriditas, now offer labyrinth facilitator training workshops, and one can locate labyrinth architecture firms and labyrinth accessories with a simple web search. See www.labyrinthlocator.com

When I was pursuing my doctorate, I used a large canvas labyrinth set up in a high-trafficked area of campus to introduce the concept to my classmates. As I demonstrated, curious undergraduates drifted by with questioning expressions. Some lingered, acting as inconspicuously as possible. This experience confirmed my inclination that the labyrinth might be an intriguing experience for curious millennials who prize participation and engagement in their spirituality.[32] Indeed, the labyrinth has been known to be "...the silent bridge between the traditional and untraditional, all the more effective...because it is nonverbal,"[33] which may well be what the passing students intuited awaited them within. I discovered that there was a, albeit sheepish, curiosity and thus the potential to draw in young adults due to the labyrinth's novelty, but I also knew I would have to create a compelling cause for them to take the time to give it a try given the constant activity that effused all their lives.

Consequently, I varied my approach to introducing the labyrinth walking experience: with some groups I spoke about the Greek myth of the Minotaur, and with others I told of the indigenous pre-Christian ritual usage, and with still others, I simply invited walkers to set an intention, engage in the walk, and then report their experiences. Ultimately, no matter the prelude to their taking the walk, compelling dialogue always surfaced, as we will soon explore.

---

32   Leonard Sweet, *Post-Modern Pilgrims: First Century Passion for the 21st Century* World (Nashville: Broadman and Holman Publishers, 2000), 190.

33   McCullogh, David Willis. The Unending Mystery: A Journey Through Mazes and Labyrinths. New York: Pantheon Books, 2004), 168.

The Labyrinth in the College Application Process

As I discussed in the last chapter, I propose that the college paradigm should be shifted, that the application/search process be viewed as a sacred journey for adolescents, and that the labyrinth is a helpful kinesthetic learning activity to assist students going through that process. What I have discovered, in my experience and research, is that not only did this kinesthetic activity allow students to make the connection between their current confusion and a larger search for identity and purpose, it provided a student-centered vehicle with "... all the time and space to reach more sophisticated levels of abstraction."[34] That is, not only can students begin to experience the healing power of a moving meditation, but they are also able to consider larger life issues relative to their current life questions or crises.

Kathryn Milun, in her book *Pathologies of Modern Space: Empty Space, Urban Anxiety, and the Recovery of the Public Self*, further corroborates the connection between kinesthetics and metaphor (emphasis mine):

> It is a very powerful experience. Walking the labyrinth is a form of kinesthetic knowledge. It allows my patients to feel their experience and to begin thinking about their life metaphorically. They come to understand that the **process** is the **journey**, not the **goal**. In the process they learn to think intuitively, to use metaphor, to feel and inhabit their own body again.[35]

She goes on to say, walking the labyrinth is "...the physical act of doing something that brings the insight," not thinking. "You don't

---

34   Ibid., 3.
35   Milun, 238.

always have to know consciously first."[36] This reiterates the essence of the multiple intelligence theory mentioned earlier, in that those who achieve insight through physical activity are equally as intelligent as those who achieve it through intellect. But more importantly, not only do different people have different learning styles predominantly, but we all have access to those we do not use predominantly and some of them are pre-abstraction, like movement, which allows us to circumvent over-analysis to achieve insight. Milun cites the experience of French philosopher and psychoanalyst Luce Irigaray and what she has learned from her practice of yoga to elucidate the bias of Western verbal communication and reasoning toward the intellect rather than proprioception.

> To tell the truth, my first encounter with a yoga teacher, which was rather conflictual, took place around the possibility of everything becoming conscious, as he declared to his students. As a psychoanalyst, I made him understand his naïveté. I could not see my own! And no more the fact that we were speaking starting from two different horizons. The practice of respiration, the practice of diverse kinds of breathing certainly reduces the darkness or the shadows of Western consciousness. But above all it constitutes the mental in a different way. It grants more attention to the education of the body, of the senses. It reverses in a way the essential and the superfluous. We Westerners believe that the essential part of culture resides in words, in texts, or perhaps in works of art, and that physical exercise should help us to dedicate ourselves to this essential. For the masters

---

36   Ibid.

of the East, the body itself can become spirit through the cultivation of breathing. Without doubt, at the origin of our tradition—for Aristotle, for example, and still more for Empedocles—the soul still seems related to the breath, to air.[37]

Reversing the essential and the superfluous is an excellent way to gesture toward how both Irigaray and I approach our respective archetypes, which both originated in inherently distinct worldviews from our own intellectual, modernism-tainted biases. Modern scholars tend to devalue that which cannot be quantified through modern metrics, but some theologians, like Leonard Sweet, argue that emotional connections and images are making a comeback in America. When so many of the young people with whom I work report struggling because of an excessive emphasis on external measures of self-worth (like gaining acceptance to prestigious colleges), never has there been a more poignant time to use a tool like labyrinth walking, which allows them to bypass cultural and other expectations in favor of exploring their own inner landscape by virtue of separating themselves from the external landscape. "Labyrinth walking focuses on mind/body connections and makes undervalued surplus sensibility a part of the healing process bringing new insight into an otherwise inexplicable sensation or behavior."[38]

Moreover, not only is realization of a new self available via labyrinth walking, but so too is discovering, and thereby overcoming to some degree, negative emotions that might be suppressed because of past trauma. "Labyrinth walking is an alternative modality that

---

37   Ibid., 234.
38   Ibid.

uses an undervalued, kinesthetic sensibility and elevates it into an authoritative mode of knowing."[39]

Even Milun, a trained psychiatrist, believes in the value of "kinesthetic knowledge, experimental knowing, feeling and inhabiting one's body again... It makes sense that physical and emotional trauma may settle into patterns that are inaccessible to the conscious self and...a wounded person may need to learn new, nonverbal, kinesthetic skills to reopen this dimension of their humanity..."[40]

While I was facilitating a labyrinth walk at Hippocrates Health Institute in Boca Raton, Florida, a woman was rendered speechless after her walk. All she could do was weep for twenty minutes, after which her only comment was: "This experience was worth the entire cost of my stay." I was so gratified to hear this—partially because I am aware of the exorbitant cost associated with a stay at the institute but mostly because I was confident that this woman had likely allowed herself to connect with a wound that may have been otherwise inaccessible. It is precisely this type of response that many people report following labyrinth walking that encouraged me to create opportunities to incorporate it into my work with clients.

39   Ibid., 244.
40   Ibid., 240.

PART TWO: REACHING THE CENTER

CHAPTER FOUR

A Mind Full

When I speak about using the labyrinth archetype as a meditative or spiritual practice for students applying to college, I speak from experience. I earned my Doctor of Ministry degree in 2015, and my dissertation was comprised of research I conducted between January and June of 2014. As part of that process, I designed three research events: one at St. Andrew's School in Boca Raton, Florida that March, one at Rabun Gap-Nacoochee School in Rabun Gap, Georgia in April, and one at the Upper Room Spiritual Center in Neptune, New Jersey in May. These research events were experiences that took place in either half- or full-day sessions, including both the labyrinth walking experience and time to debrief.

My goal was to design a sanctuary for the adolescent demographic, and I began with the concept of the pilgrimage as the unifying narrative of my project. This evolved into a growing concern with what I believed is a lack of centeredness in students and, more broadly, adolescents in general. I then chose to expand the pilgrimage metaphor by incorporating the walking labyrinth as the experiential component of my project. However, after conducting my first research opportunity, it became evident to me that the juniors and seniors (who were seventeen and eighteen years old) I studied represent only part of the journey since, by this age, they are nearing the culmination of it. I then expanded my research subjects to include younger high school teens.

The schedule of the research events went like this: I facilitated labyrinth walks for each group, then conducted interviews that posed a series of questions, and documented the correlative narrative results. Using the lens of the labyrinth process and a six-prompt questionnaire I distributed to each participant, I wanted to ascertain whether or not applicants viewed their college process as a sacred journey. My goal in doing this was to gesture toward the value of carving out sacred space in teens' lives throughout this transitional phase in young adulthood. I aimed to call attention to the fecundity of this chaotic season in their young lives for self-discovery, development, and personal mastery as well as for possible encounters with the divine (although pilgrimage is not exclusively a phenomenon associated with religion, that was part of the auspices for my research). This project was intended to create the space to allow each participant to interpret the experience of the search and application process as viewed through the lens of the labyrinth, and it was also intended simply to give them the opportunity to experience silence and inward reflection, opportunities, as stated, that are rare for boarding school students.

Some of the students' responses were about experiencing feeling lost and disoriented in the application process, and equally many of their responses post-walk were about feeling lost in the labyrinth. The labyrinth then emerged as a means to explore the sensation of lostness as a psychological state betwixt and between senses of self in a secure yet meaningful way. The participants readily recognized lostness as a psychological state but also as a metaphor for abiding between states of being that are more easily defined and therefore accepted, like high school student and college student, in favor of accepting change as life itself and life as change.

Themes surrounding the states of being lost and found abound in sacred literature. From the wilderness wandering of the Israelites in the Book of Exodus to the gone-missing adolescent Jesus, disorientation and the emotions that accompany loss and being lost surface as human beings recognize their inherent nature to wander in the psychological sense, moving constantly from one role of sense of self to another.

Loss is a profound emotion. In the face of being lost in the woods as a child, and of briefly losing my own young daughter as a parent, I felt utterly devoid of power over the situation. As a child, I ran further into the forest, fueled by fear. As an adult, the reality of my daughter's disappearance left me screaming her name, desperately scrambling about before collapsing from grief. These horrifying and torturous feelings are ones from which anyone would rightly flee. Walter Bruggemann, in *The Psalms and the Life of Faith*, offers an approach to organizing the psalms that highlights three distinct movements: orientation, disorientation, and new or reorientation. The latter is signified by such terms as surprise and gift.[41]

The correlation to the three movements of the labyrinth, the three stages of rites of passage, and also the theory of positive disintegration (in which a conception must be relinquished in order for a transformed one to emerge) is obvious. This is what makes the use of the labyrinth so appealing: historically, the earliest labyrinths predate Christianity, and in recent years they have re-entered popular culture and are found in New Age circles. As such, the labyrinth

---

41 Bruggemann, Walter. The Psalms and the Life of Faith. Philadelphia: Fortress Press, 1995.)Pew Research Center, 2014.

can be (and often is) used as a faith-neutral meditative aid, and the crux of my project was figuring out how to make the process seeker-sensitive for the largely "spiritual but not religious" audience of postmodern American youth. In my research project, the labyrinth gave me the benefit of using an ancient and future tool that allowed the students to use that lens to see that everything is a work in progress, that change is truly the only certainty, and feeling lost is not to be evaded or shunned but accepted as an opportunity for growth.

The labyrinth is also effective because it engages students at a profoundly physical level: students see the pattern below and before them, walk the path with often-bare feet, and hear either music used to set the mood or the brooks, wind, trees, and birds in nature. I can certainly attest to having my senses of taste and smell heghtened in my own experiences walking the labyrinth, and this heightened reconnection with the senses is one of the conditions prompted by walking the labyrinth that allows for the achievement of a more contemplative, reflective state.

Once this mindfulness begins to take root, walkers are welcomed to wander the twisting path and become voluntarily disoriented, lost, which as noted previously can be radically positive if the facilitator uses it to yield insight and as a metaphor to frame life's transitions. In essence, the labyrinth can be a safe way to explore the sensation of lostness in a meaningful way and thereby unlock the possibility to broach, unpack, and potentially restructure a period of transition in a way that fosters the acceptance of change as fundamental to life itself.

Centering and Interior Footwork

The same terms from my narratives of loss and being lost, terms like panicked, frustrated, anxious, alone, abandoned, despair, and disbelief echo throughout my students' questionnaire responses. What these terms indicated to me was an absence of centeredness in my young clients.

The former director of choral activities for Westminster Choir College in Princeton, New Jersey, Dr. Joseph Flummerfelt, addressed the concept of the center during his graduation address to the class of 1989:

> He is seated in his (sic) own center—a man who flows from his core and therefore from the center of life. A man who is integrated, a man who lives life from the inside out, who knows and is at one with himself. I think one of the great sicknesses of the human condition today is the extent to which we are estranged from ourselves, the extent to which we clamor after gurus of whatever ilk, be they TV preachers, political demagogues, paperback therapists, or the requisite name on the back side of our blue jeans, to tell us who we are, what to believe, what to think, indeed even to tell us that we exist. Far too many of us look outside ourselves for our center, for our sense of being... Lacking connection with our own centers, we lack the capacity to penetrate to the center of that which is about us.

In other words, very few people have sufficient comfort in their own identity beyond outside influences, which include media of all kinds and the strong tendency toward peer approval, to live their lives unencumbered by external pressures to conform or perform, to live as if claiming their inalienable right to the pursuit of their own happiness.

I have discovered in my own research and throughout my two decades of work with adolescents that it is the rare teen who has achieved advanced self-knowledge through being in touch with their center, who has achieved identity apart from the myriad influences of others. A strong sense of self requires deliberate work—work which requires silence and reflection. Not only are all of those external influences, which one might think of in the aggregate as noise, keeping the young from seeking a sense of self that allows them to be centered, but the lack of any reflection does as well. In short, this very deliberate work of becoming centered requires a person to seek out an absence of "noise" and to actually seek self-knowledge and, perhaps thereby, wisdom. For as Aristotle said, "Know thyself. It is the beginning of all wisdom."

This lack of access to silence and a willingness to reflect means walking the labyrinth can cause polarized responses among students. Some teens may feel daunted by the prospect of becoming quiet and looking within for self-definition while others welcome the opportunity and are soothed by the practice. According to author and composer Ned Rorem in *Setting the Tone*, "Listening is easy. But true ease, like anything worthwhile, may be hard to cultivate. We hear all the time, even in sleep, though we don't always listen to what we hear."[42] To listen attentively to a deeper, more profound voice than those bombarding us daily from outside, that still small voice of wisdom, we need to quiet down, slow down, and turn our attention inward.

The power of the labyrinth is in fact its place within the liminal, as a map of sorts that is not of the world but of the self. As Gernot Candolini, labyrinth architect and researcher notes in his work *Labyrinths: Walking Toward the Center*, a detailed pilgrimage to many

---

42 Ned Rorem, *Setting the Tone: Essays and a Diary* (New York: Open Road Integrated Media, 1983), 312.

of the historical European labyrinth sites, "The center is where we encounter…inner and outer monsters." His book, part field guide and part personal journal, recounts his journey in a camper with his wife and young daughter, visiting with labyrinth experts and trying to elucidate the mysterious labyrinth's draw for him. He muses: "But I've been toying with another thought as well. The center is also where the encounter with the Minotaur occurs, a confrontation with the self, the battle with the inner and outer monsters."[43]

Candolini's journey, and subsequent construction of labyrinths forced him to confront the Greek myth and the metaphor of the labyrinth head-on. His insights might flow from a labyrinth that he encountered, in which the center was a chamber surrounded by mirrors with the inscription, "This is the Minotaur." Or his insights might flow from Leonardo da Vinci's sketch of the labyrinth center made up of eight linked mirrors. The first sentence in the guide book Candolini uses when he discovers the mirror labyrinth reads, "In the labyrinth, one doesn't meet the Minotaur. One meets oneself."[44]

This has provided another apt metaphor for the college application process: the process puts students in direct conflict with themselves. "Many people won't try the labyrinth," Candolini observes, "for fear of losing their way. They can't get past the notion that (they think) the labyrinth is really a maze… [They] fear the possibility of doing something wrong."[45] The question this continually raises for me is what is prompting this fear of failure? Do a sense of failure and the sensation of being lost dovetail? Is it the myth of perfection that gives rise to this fear? Is it the fear of not having a clear, unobstructed view of the goal that gives rise to a fear of failure?

---

43 Candolini, 77.

44 Ibid., 5.

45 Ibid., 78.

I have seen this fear in some of my clients, but then there are clients who are so paralyzed by a different kind of fear—of making a mistake—that they never choose at all. I call this paralysis by over analysis. What people who avoid the labyrinth do not realize is that lost is only what the labyrinth represents. Lost is in fact what they already are, and moreover, there is not a wrong turn to be made: only a path to tread in search of self.

At the labyrinth walk I facilitated at the Hippocrates Health Institute, I encountered another woman who was utterly afraid to walk the labyrinth. "I am afraid of getting lost," she told me. I attempted to empathize despite my not understanding (to me, the fear of getting lost in a walking labyrinth inlaid in the ground is like someone saying they cannot walk through sprinklers because they are afraid of drowning). I offered her a hand-held finger labyrinth, a wooden circle with grooves carved in the pattern of a labyrinth to trace, but she could not even do that with her eyes closed, her fear of becoming lost was so paralyzing, and I had a hunch that she had experienced something traumatic that had left fear as its legacy.

The next day I followed up with her one-on-one. "From where might your fear of being lost originate?"

She replied, "As a child, my older sisters locked me in a dark closet once. I was so panicked. I was trapped in there for some time before I was let out. Perhaps this could be one trigger." I suggested that perhaps some part of her subconscious throws her into a panic rather than allow her to discover what it is she is not ready to face.

I once had a client who could not close off any of her options. She participated in her high school's International Baccalaureate program and was superior in the humanities but preferred the sciences because she wanted to be a doctor. Whenever we seemed to accomplish a milestone, like finalizing a college list or deciding on an essay topic, she second-guessed herself, saying she wanted to start over. I finally asked her, "Do you think you might have trust issues?" Ever since I posed the question, she has begun to think about that possibility. Recently, halfway down the stairs out of my office, she said, "I really trust your opinion, Erin." The overt and intricate link between fear and trust in the college process had now emerged for exploration.

Candolini writes, "If life is viewed as a maze, every mistake is an unnecessary detour and a waste of time. If life is a labyrinth, then every mistake is a part of the path and an indispensable master teacher."[46] I have tried to encourage my students, the ones who are plagued by the fear of making the wrong decision or getting lost and having to turn back, that each step of the journey is meaningful and there are no wrong choices—except deciding not to choose at all. I then remind them of the concept of liminality, that the wild edges of that field is where all of the growth and action can take place, outside of the realm of the orderly and familiar. Candolini once more:

> This desire for certainty can also make the path in the labyrinth difficult. First, it swings to the left, then to the right. Everything changes: perspective, direction, movement. What was hitherto clear may now no longer be relevant; something that had finally come into perspective may no longer make sense. But if I'm forced, midcourse, to give up something familiar that I've relied on to get where I am, I'll be willing to accept the change as long as it is clear that it is helping me to move forward. I'll want this turn in the path to at least lead me inward,

---

46 Ibid., 50.

toward the center. But if the turn leads instead outward, I grow frustrated. Can this be right? The longing for what I'm used to grows. I get vexed with the world that won't stand still.[47]

Many years ago, while reading Robert James Waller's *The Bridges of Madison County*, I recall being struck by Robert Kincaid's observation, "Things change. They always do, it's one of the things of nature. Most people are afraid of change, but if you look at it as something you can always count on, then it can be a comfort."[48] Perhaps the nomads I have met, those who have a certain comfort level with encountering the unknown, have made that paradigmatic shift from fearing difference and the unknown to embracing the fact that the only certainty is that the future is a mystery. Even those who fail to choose might one day realize the psychological truth in the metaphor of the labyrinth: that if they are to go boldly, seeking the life they desire, they need to accept that life is not a series of guarantees but rather a decision tree with many potential pathways. Most certainly, many of my clients realize, after their experience inside the labyrinth, that the number of choices available in life approaches infinity and thus mistakes are both inevitable and a treasure-trove of learning and growth opportunities—and so too the much smaller but still important decision regarding college matriculation.

Dis-orientation

Most young children have enjoyed a piñata at a party. A child traditionally is blindfolded, given a stick and spun around several times to increase the disorientation. Then the child is left to swing wildly

---

47   Ibid., 102-103.

48   Waller, Robert James, The Bridges of Madison County. (New York: Warner Publishing, 1992), 246.

at the perceived target strung up high and often on a pulley system that allows the target to be altered. Onlookers laugh, perhaps nervously knowing their turn is approaching, at the entertainment of observing the swinger's random attempts at success. Children derive enjoyment from rising to the challenge of this seemingly impossible task because they view it as a game. They are at ease with the disorientation as simply part of the challenge.

Student responses indicate that the labyrinth's serpentine meandering can create a simulation of the disorientation often caused by confrontation of the unknown, which in turn increases applicants' threshold for disorientation and allows them to embrace the unknown as simply part of the challenge. Thus freed, students will be less distracted by fear of the unknown and walk boldly into the center where each can confront and embrace the self. This is, very succinctly stated, the purpose of walking the labyrinth.

I'm amused by the irony that walking the labyrinth feels like a winding path and yet the result is often described as an "unwinding." Perhaps the labyrinth walk can be viewed as an "unwinding" of the many outside layers enveloping the subconscious that keep a person from exploring the deeply unsettling mystery of the self.

In Chapter One, we detailed the disconnect resulting from the panopticon effect of social media inundating young people with unrelenting images of peer success, accomplishment, and the perception of constant, though contrived, enjoyment and fun. Our social media-saturated culture has emphasized looking outward and judging one's self compared to others. The labyrinth is a tool that grants permission to students to detach from this bombardment of messages and to look inward. When a student who chooses to enter the labyrinth reaches the center, this is a symbolic achievement of centeredness; and if a person is firmly centered in their own skin and personal purpose, outside influences have less hold on their psyche.

So often in literature, film, and other media, the culminating confrontation is frequently between the protagonist and him/herself. That is, the dramatic action entails a struggle from within, which as film or literature is a heightened form of life writ large. That is, our artistic presentations represent the true struggle for us all: the individual with him/herself within some context that sets the stage for the confrontation.

Perhaps this is why da Vinci's labyrinth has a mirror center. It is only in the act of quieting and reducing the din of distractions (like anger and fear of abandonment) that an individual has the opportunity to commune with themselves, and at the center of the labyrinth, that is what they encounter. We now see the indispensability of silence in achieving centeredness. According to Dr. Flummerfelt in another comment to Westminster graduates:

If asked to describe one of my most important growth concerns, I would answer that we become more fully alive by finding and maintaining a vital connection with the creative pulse of life. Some of you may call this impulse "God," some "the spiritual source," some "the creative center"… This also means learning to listen. To listen deeply. To listen to the song within. To silence the clatter of the cognitive brain and learn to be in the moment. Then we will have the possibility of hearing our own intuitive, spontaneous voice—that powerful still small voice which comes from the same impulse that generates all creation.

Flummerfelt refers to the still, small voice mentioned in the Christian bible that is the voice of God, but it can be considered in secular psychological terms, as well, as the voice of our own interior wisdom, a voice that is both prior to rumination and reasoning and a result of it but at a more profound, and perhaps unconscious, level. Centering oneself is perhaps the most profound achievement of walking the labyrinth.

As the Turners selected several traditional pilgrimage locations for the purposes of their research, I have selected narratives from the separate settings in which I collected my research, and I explore in the sections that follow the variety of sacred journeys of self-discovery, as well as the shadow script (the darker, terror-inducing thoughts and emotions) shared by those actively engaged in the college selection process. I share these pieces of narrative research to show just how this act of walking the labyrinth has allowed not only students but other stakeholders, in the college process and beyond, to access a deep source within themselves, which actively opened these individuals to profound reflections that allowed them to access a well of inner strength to process past obstacles and identity issues.

CHAPTER FIVE

This Time Around

Chronicles of St. Andrew's School, FL

Early-morning classes breed taciturn teenagers. This worked to my advantage at St. Andrew's School in Boca Raton, Florida, which I visited during the "Spiritual Journey Days" that immediately preceded spring break. The students spoke little in their groggy states, but in the labyrinth, they soon began moving and immersing themselves in the experience.

I selected St. Andrew's because of the on-campus labyrinth. Today you are as apt to find walking labyrinths in schools, hospitals, prisons, and public parks as you might find them in places of worship. This outdoor labyrinth was constructed at the request of a former administrator and ordained Episcopal priest who envisioned it to be used in disciplinary matters, allowing students to process the outcomes of decisions they had made. The idea was that students who had broken a school rule or acted in an inappropriate way in class would take the time to walk the labyrinth to reflect on their choices and thereby identify what might have triggered such behavior and what might be done to avoid repeating it. I thought this an excellent way to foster both self awareness in individual students and a disciplinary system focused on raising self awareness. The administrator later left the school, and the labyrinth went largely underutilized thereafter. Perhaps there were fewer disciplinary issues to address. Perhaps the idea seemed too time-consuming. Or maybe the idea was simply abandoned all together. After all, a swift detention should be a sufficient deterrent to future infractions, shouldn't it?

The upperclassmen I studied all walked the labyrinth twice. The restless goofing off demonstrated by this class during their first labyrinth walk the day prior morphed into a sacred, silent procession as I led them into the labyrinth. I have learned that pace-setting vitally impacts the communal experience, and so I led them deliberately but not overly slowly. Amazingly, they kept silent for the full twenty-minute walking experience. When we exited, we took our seats on beach towels around the perimeter of this outdoor labyrinth. I turned off the music and began to debrief.

I asked them how the experience felt the second day compared to the day before. *Different*, one responded. Others chimed in. *Nice. Faster.* I then asked, "When in your day, if at all, do you experience such a swath of silence?" *During tests*, they responded. *Doing homework. Running.* I thought about how rare simple silence is for these students, how there is no allotted time when they were not being bombarded by noise and images and commitments. Next I asked if anyone had reflected further on how the labyrinth related to their college journey. One boy said, "I realized I don't really want to go to the college I chose, and that I'm going to transfer as soon as possible." I thought, *What an epiphany!*

By then the chaplain had joined us and asked, "Might there be any significance to the twists and turns in today's labyrinth experience?"

One student interrupted. "They represent change. But everything is changing. If it weren't, there would be no future; everything would be the same."

Another student expressed her perception of the reality of competition: "We are competing with each other [in the college application process.]" The shadow script emerges, I noted: "Yeah, where you live and how much money you have helps you in getting into college. Some people have it easier...and some harder."

"Today kids have to grow up faster," observed another student. "It was way easier in past generations."

The chaplain left us with a parting thought: "There is a difference between knowing the path and walking the path." I inquired as to the source of the quote later and found it was from the film *The Matrix*. The line is from the very suspenseful scene in which the Oracle informed the hero, Neo, that he is not "the One," the savior figure. Yet we learn that Neo is only told what he needs to be told in order to realize his true identity as the One. The chaplain seemed to challenge the students to distinguish between having the knowledge of what will come and simply trusting themselves and the process, relinquishing any attempt to control the outcome even if that was only obsessing about how things should turn out.

I asked the students if they'd had prior experiences with the St. Andrew's labyrinth. Many had never experienced it even though it had been in the same place on the back of campus property, adjacent to the chapel and across from the middle school building, for a decade. Many had no idea it even existed. Three of the students who had been at St. Andrew's since middle school recalled having experiences with it back then. I pressed further, about school cohesion and one student said, "Seniors have a day once per year when they pair off with a Kindergartener. We have a lunch with them. The higher grade students have no connection to the lower school besides that."

"What about new-student orientation?" I asked. The same faculty member apparently gives the same orientation presentation every year, the students told me. I suggested implementing a labyrinth walk as part of these activities at the beginning of each school year. Students also shared with me that, in the past, residential students had used the labyrinth as an exit ritual before graduation.

I then inquired about the chaplain's earlier point and asked them about the twists and turns in the labyrinth. They spoke freely: "In order to get to your destination, you have to move back and forth. I wanted to cut corners. I was relieved when it was over."

Describe the experience: "long, eye-opening, good" were all the responses I received.

I revisited the experience later with another group. "I felt like I was spinning. You need patience with the spinning and quick turns and continuing. In the beginning, I was thinking about something and I felt stuck. By halfway, I wasn't stuck anymore."

When I invited the students to share advice with younger students about the college process, they had much to say: "I would have tried harder in school. Try not to stress. Apply to more schools. Start early with your applications. Start thinking about your extracurriculars earlier."

These discussions begin to reveal how the labyrinth can serve as symbol for the personal journey and a quiet space for reflection. It is precisely the silence that allows for the inward inquiry, the movement stimulates kinesthetic learning and the collective activity enables the sense of communitas as students carve out time to come together and be attentive to their need to unwind, to vent and share.

Living Out Loud

I was struck by the fact that each senior knew where everyone else in their class had been accepted to college. They knew where, and even whether, other members of the group had been admitted. They were also able to connect the dots between their fellow students various activities to figure out what the golden admission ticket might have been for each.

It occurred to me then that being a teenager today really means living out loud; that is, thanks to social media their identities and accomplishments seem to exist in the public domain. When I asked these seniors to offer advice to underclassmen, the final piece of advice was: "Have fun."

"I applied to twelve schools and wrote twenty separate essays," observed one girl. "I showed my essay to many people and I got shot down several times."

"Every night, half of my work was college related."

"Walking helps you to think if you get stuck."

"I can see how silence can help with decision making."

All of these responses seem to corroborate that the students were beginning to dig deeper into the very process from which they had just emerged—many not unscathed.

More students joined in the labyrinth experience as the week progressed and the word got out. Students shouted out descriptive words in response to my query: *cleansing, calming, dizzying, confusing, scary, soothing, relaxing, peaceful, focusing.* When I asked how and why the Minotaur could be imprisoned in a labyrinth that has only one way out, a student declared, "Because you can't see it coming. You have no idea." I had discussed with students the concept of the labyrinth prior to these walks, correlating the history, which included the Greek version and the characters of Theseus and the Minotaur and the labyrinth as a mysterious hidden prison, with the symbolic and psychological. In short, the students were familiar with the story by the time they walked their labyrinth, and this student's comment reveals discomfort with uncertainty and unease regarding the possibility of surprises along the journey. When I asked how a labyrinth differs from a maze, many students said that one can get lost or make wrong turns in a maze and be forced to turn around. One student shared, "The object of the maze is to think. The object of the labyrinth is to walk." These intuitive realizations began to surface in our debriefing talks, evidencing the students' deep desire to process the experience and to connect it to their own experiences.

Prior to some of the walks, I posed questions about students' associations with the labyrinth. Students' answers frequently referenced Ariadne, who gave Theseus a spool of thread to help him find his way back out. I asked the students, "What about the significance of Ariadne's thread?" The thread represented a comfort for one student, a way out for another. One student shared that he liked "[not having] to think…just [focusing] on a topic." Another enjoyed the chance to concentrate.

Another question broached the notion of communitas: How did you feel about how you were in relation to each other when you were walking the labyrinth? "I felt like we had the same destination, but we're just at different stages of the journey. I couldn't tell if they were ahead of me or behind me because of all the switchbacks. Somehow, it didn't matter." In short, the students began to release their need to compare themselves to others and to recognize their shared journey.

Another student added, "I felt like I was in a trance." When I asked her to expound, she observed, "I began to see the walk as a puzzle. It is made of different sized bricks and I began to focus on my foot steps and on the shapes of the bricks and making patterns with the stones I chose to place my feet on." This seemed to free the student to obtain a deeper state of meditation.

"Did you get lost in thought?" Another student asked. "A few times, I felt confused, like, was I on this path before? I don't remember being in this spot on the way in."

"I felt not quite ever there yet. I was close [to the center], but as you get close, you turn away again."

"What was the hardest part?" I asked.

She replied, "Walking straight for the long stretch then having to turn was the hardest for me." For her, that represented "the crazy versus the calm times" in life.

After school on the third day of my research event, faculty members Becky and Tim arrived to walk the labyrinth. I offered some cursory reflections regarding the labyrinth and sent them in. Afterward, we gathered under the trees. The chaplain offered, "This was cleansing, calming. After meeting everyone else's needs and reading that last email from a disgruntled parent, this was a peaceful and relaxing way to release the day's tension."

Next, Tim: "I was trying not to anticipate the turns. I was simply being mindful of each step, deliberately slowing down my pace, intentionally noticing details."

"Like the heat of the stones on my feet," added Becky, who had never walked the labyrinth barefoot before that day.

This reaffirmed for me the power of such sacred space and of silence in these participants' lives.

I asked them about their ideas for increased usage of the labyrinth within the school community. Becky shared that she would like to take her students there before exams, musing, "I'd like to get them away from the frantic and into the focus." However, she questioned whether there could ever be any spare time made in the schedule.

The chaplain suddenly dropped a proverbial bomb on our conversation: the school's long-term planning committee had been discussing paving over the grove where the labyrinth lay to use the space for a parking lot. He remarked, "This sense of immediacy is real... We must honor the gift [of the labyrinth]." I echoed that sentiment, and I commented on the extreme rarity of a school with a labyrinth before promising to make professional recommendations regarding ideas for increased use. There is no doubt of teens' need for such spaces at this juncture in life, I told the others, and it concerns me that what few exist are apparently at risk. The loss of all sense of centering could mean certain calamity for our culture.

I also noted the tension of walking the labyrinth with others. The pace of those walking ahead seemed to be a detail that caused the group to reflect on their own pace of life and desire for individual expression.

One participant observed: "In the walk yesterday, some classes looked like a line of ants, following along after the one before rather than making one's own pace and decisions. When I walked it last night with the leader who set an exceedingly slow pace, I too, followed the pace to fit in, but I experienced my own desire for a different pace."

When discussing the labyrinth metaphorically, Tim and the chaplain felt that they were "journeying on the way out" at this stage in their lives. Becky countered, "I always feel like I am on the way in. Perhaps it's my personality type."

The next day the varsity football quarterback took the lead into the labyrinth when I invited another class to walk it. As I frequently do, I began the session by describing the labyrinth as a lens that can be used to look within oneself. The group arrived in the middle of the labyrinth and enjoyed some time in the silence, and at the end, they gathered in a huddle, arms linked and heads bowed. They shared that the college process is focused more on grades and statistics and less on the person. One student, who is decidedly not going to college immediately after high school, focused on this question: "What will make me happy?"

The football player observed, "The twists and turns are all about footwork."

I asked the students, "If the labyrinth is a timeline of your life, where are you?"

A student responded, "In the beginning, going through the roughest part."

Another replied, "It'll be a new start at college… A new beginning, maybe a whole new labyrinth."

I followed up with, "If high school has been its own labyrinth experience, then where are you?"

"We have to get out!" said one student, referring to this being senior year, and laughter erupted.

"If you could do something over in high school, what would it be?"

One student would have come to this school a year sooner. Some international students would have spent more time working on their English skills and been more knowledgeable about American culture. One might have taken the SAT earlier. Another wished he'd liked high school more.

A group of boisterous upperclassmen entered the labyrinth. As they began the walk, there was a palpable tone of horseplay, so much talking as they embarked on the path. I watched and waited. At the center, a bottleneck occurred and one boy jostled another. As they progressed, I overheard among the chatter:

"Is anyone else getting a bit dizzy?"

"I'm getting lost."

"Am I ever going to reach the middle?"

"Man, that took a while."

"This is taking forever!"

"Am I going backward?"

"I'm so close [to the center of the labyrinth]! Why can't I just get there?"

"Has this thing [the labyrinth] always been here?"

Community Stakeholders Converge

The evening walk was not with students but other important people in the St. Andrew's community: Nadia, the parent of a student, along with her two adult step-daughters Sarah and Mary; a physics teacher and his ten-year-old daughter Emma; and Claire, another parent of a student.

One of Nadia's daughters, a yoga instructor, started the walk at a deliberate pace: heel-toe, heel-toe. Sarah and Mary walked before her. They shared some time in the middle. Emma came behind Claire. I vacillated: should I ask Emma to just pass Claire? I let it be. When we debriefed, Claire shared that having Emma's shadow come in front of her was the moment of the walk that spoke the most to her.

"Peaceful, quiet, and gentle" were the first descriptors I received during our discussion. "Surprising, fun, cleansing, filtering" came next. "Refreshing after a day like this," someone added. "When you walk, it's like peeling the onion. At the center, you are refreshed, and you can then take that with you."

I observed how crucial the pace was in this walk experience. The chaplain had joined us and chose not to walk. He'd commented that the walkers appeared to be moving so slowly and he was self-aware enough to know that he was not in the mood to downshift to this slower, meditative speed. Another of the walkers shared that, at one point, she just had to step out of the path. "I realized I needed to just be and not do." One added that she appreciated the rhythm of her experience versus the erratic steps she had taken earlier that day.

The walkers also recognized the simplicity of observing one's foot connected to the ground and feeling the air on one's skin. Sarah shared, "It's like an accordion. The labyrinth expands as if to create more space."

The labyrinth pleasantly surprised Mary. She talked about the business she had started with her husband after the financial crises of the past several years, and how she struggled with wanting to be certain of outcomes in an uncertain time. She said that, while she was walking, she thought, *"All I can do is walk the path,"* meaning as she journeyed through this tumultuous time. Mary tried to impart life lessons to her younger brother, a high-achieving eighth-grader, and told him that the path is anything but linear. She had earned her degrees and did everything "right," but her path, too, was anything but linear. In short, she believed the lack of linearity is the hallmark of adulthood, and dealing with this reality is the measure of success.

The lower school chaplain, Faye, suggested using the labyrinth as a "cooling-off" spot for students with behavioral issues. Sarah thought it could be used in lieu of punishment or for ceremonial rites of passage. "Many students set goals and say, if they can just get that to goal, it will be the end and they will be happy. Like, we don't tell myths to teach kids that monsters exist, we tell them so they learn that they can be overcome, conquered. So could the labyrinth be used to remedy or reduce test anxiety?" In fact, the school had recently brought in a speaker to address anxiety. He spoke on cognitive behavior for kids who stress. He ended his talk with the serenity prayer, which is essentially a letting go exercise. The takeaway was that anxiety is okay and the key is learning how to cope. So, Sarah's suggestion seems spot on.

Nadia focused on slowing down, hearing people, and avoiding having an agenda in her conversations. The upper school chaplain had a realization about the parental function in stress-making. I suggested that my experience revealed that students echo the stress of the parents. He recognized that there is such a difference between applying to college when their parents did it and now. More ideas surfaced as to how best to use the sacred space the labyrinth represents, such as peer leadership or perhaps integrating the three schools better. One person asked, "Could the college process begin with this walking experience to allow students to think more about the fit with a given school?" The residential life program could own the labyrinth, someone else suggested, to emphasize the concept of "journey." The two chaplains both spoke to balancing "sales" and "souls." St. Andrew's School is a rigorous college feeder. I shared the observation that we are valuing teens for what they *do* more than for whom they are—and the tragedy is that they know it.

"Adults project our own personal path onto our children. This exercise could help adults see that our children have their own path," I told them. Mary observed that, when she was in middle school, she never thought about college. Today, students are thinking about it at least that early in their education. I was then told a story of a young boy who was reduced to tears after requesting extended time on a test, and when he relinquished the test, he blubbered, "I'll never get into Columbia Law!" He was 11.

Sarah told the group about quitting her communications job at the United Nations to teach yoga fulltime and how people received this news. Perhaps the labyrinth disarms in order to engage, I thought. "The labyrinth has its own intelligence" was one of the final comments made by one of the adult walkers. And as will soon become clear, students can and will connect with the labyrinth's intelligence in a deep and profound way.

CHAPTER SIX

The Longest Possible Route in the Most Compact Space

Chronicles of Rabun Gap-Nacoochee School

Before going into private practice, I spent much of my career in boarding schools; but I had never visited Rabun Gap-Nacoochee School prior to my research trip. A colleague in campus ministry, Rev. Jeffrey Reynolds, was the longtime chaplain at Rabun Gap, and he invited me to conduct my research there. He mentioned the classical labyrinth just miles up the road from campus and how he had somehow made efforts to incorporate it into his lesson plans for the religious studies classes he taught. I thought that, since the scope of my project focused on the college process, my visit could be a way to introduce the labyrinth archetype to the school's college counseling staff.

In my mind's eye, perhaps due to the indigenous nature of its name and its location in remote northern Georgia, I associated it with dirt roads and rural resources. But the school looked identical to any elite New England boarding school except located in the South! I gawked as I took in the school on a hill surrounded by mountain views and bucolic fields, manicured lawns and babbling brooks. The state-of-the-art facilities belied a school of twice the enrollment, and yet they had lavished all of this on a mere two hundred high schoolers. I sent my husband a panoramic photo of campus, and he told me it was time to go back into teaching!

For two consecutive days, with the assistance of the college counseling staff and the chaplain, we bussed students off campus to the classical walking labyrinth, which was just a few miles away on the border with North Carolina. We walked a short path over a bridge and into an opening, with a brook on one side and the labyrinth on the other. The setting is so beautiful that it felt like a retreat.

Students embarked on the walk after I invited them to reflect on their college search process at this juncture. I felt particularly justified in making this the intention of the walk because the class time I was allotted was usually reserved for their weekly college counseling meetings. During the brief ride to the labyrinth, I asked students where they had first heard of the labyrinth and, without fail, a student from each class mentioned Greek mythology and capably recounted the myth of Theseus and the Minotaur. One student retold Theseus's epic journey at length and with much detail; I was very impressed with his storytelling abilities. He went on to share, "Maybe for Theseus, the Minotaur is his feminine side. All heroes have to have courage and strength, but they also have to have a heart to lead and become a king. If not, he will become a tyrant. If he has too much heart, however, he will give away the kingdom."

A Dispatch from Within the Snow Globe

Having been both a boarding school student and faculty member (the many hats I wore included curriculum developer, dorm supervisor, tennis coach, community service coordinator, a cappella choir director, and chaplain), I have a firm grasp of how insular and all-encompassing boarding school life can be. I was tickled to hear, then, one student beginning our discussion on the lack of private reflection time with, "It's a snow globe!"

Another student followed with, "Boarding students are on campus all the time. It was nice to get off campus (to walk the labyrinth). Everything around you on campus reminds you of papers that are due." This led us into a discussion of stress in the college selection process, a topic about which everyone who participated in the research project had strong opinions.

One of the college counselors who had joined us on the walk asked the students, "You all said you were scared and stressed about college. High schoolers generally want to be independent... Our goal is to help. Does our role make it feel more stressful?"

A student replied, "The abstract concept of college is less stressful than the list of details and steps to check off, which makes me more stressed."

The counselor responded, "We give you those lists so, when we get to the end, you're not out of time and freak out. We are here to assist, not to nag." She then commiserated, "It's a daunting process."

"Having you as a help is great," added another student. "It's the reality that stresses us."

Another concurred: "Everything you give us is a huge help, and the reality check is that it's coming quick and we have to figure it out before it's too late."

The counselor said, "There must be a lot of pressure to succeed. Remember, success is finding that place where you feel comfortable about yourself and the growth you'll experience."

Listening to this, I thought about how fortunate these students are that they are surrounded by caring and empathetic adults who have not only expressed solidarity with the emotions associated with the college process but are co-journeying on it with the students. I knew that walking the labyrinth together might only amplify this sense of co-journeying.

The counselor added, "It's nice to look where you're walking and see the bumps in the road. I liked hearing the water and reading the fruits of the spirit [the one-word messages written on the rocks in the labyrinth]. The first starts with gentleness."

I realized the notable contrast between these students' reflections of the labyrinth experience and the students at St. Andrew's School the previous month. Where the St. Andrew's students were very savvy to the worldly ways to win through competition and peer approval, the Rabun Gap students presented as holistic, critical thinkers who were comfortable sharing their opinions, especially when they differ from their peers. The contrast seemed in part a function of location and socioeconomics, but this also points out the necessity of being sensitized to the differing impacts that various geographic settings have on the self-perceptions of students.

Even the Minotaur is Someone's Son

Then, I met Navi during one of the walks I facilitated at Rabun Gap. She moved deliberately around the labyrinth and took copious amounts of time in the center, and I decided to engage her one-on-one after her walk. I found her with her shoes removed and her feet in the babbling brook beside the labyrinth.

I had heard that she had all the credits she needed to graduate and was planning to leave Rabun Gap and start college online after her junior year. I asked her how she felt about leaving.

"I feel it's time to move on and expand on to newer things," she told me. "Being as independent as I've become over the last two years, I'm not too worried about it. I try not to let things like that worry me. School, I've been doing that for twelve years. I just think it's an unnecessary emphasis that people put on how hard everything has to be. It doesn't have to be hard. It's only hard if you make it hard."

"Almost like an arbitrary…"

"Yeah, like with SATs and ACTs, these huge scores… Everyone is freaking out, but it's just… You only freak out because it's how everyone else is reacting to it."

"One of the other girls was saying the same thing," I responded, "like it's a communal psychosis." I interpreted these comments as further evidence that applicants are fully aware of how detrimental the old paradigm of admissions as a zero-sum game is.

"I used to read a lot and go outside, and it's painful to not be able to do this more. I also visualize a lot."

"Did you have any questions answered in the labyrinth?"

Referencing the spool of thread given to Theseus by Ariadne in the Greek mythology of the labyrinth, Navi pondered aloud: "I like the metaphor of going in and coming out using the string. But one has to remember that the Minotaur was also someone's son. I always found it interesting that maybe it's not a beast that we have to tackle but one that we have to make friends with. So, rather than trying to slay it completely, maybe we need to try to figure out, well, why is it so angry?

"So I definitely found and asked for peace," she continued. "Book work and deadline-deadline-deadline…can be just as destructive as it is helpful. I feel like education has become a series of preparations for tests rather than choosing: 'I want to learn this.'"

91

I asked her, "If you felt like this would be beneficial, what part of the labyrinth walk would be helpful, and when, in the college search process?"

"Once in the beginning, once in the middle, and once at the end," she said. "Ask at the beginning: what do I want to get out of this? Midway through: what have I gotten out of this so far? At the end: what have I learned?"

Clearly this deep-souled student has deliberately moved into the labyrinth folklore and mythology to engage the metaphor in such a novel way. Perhaps she, too, is a nomad. Although I do not know of her past experiences with loss and being lost, she appeared to practice centering through her visualizations and showed a rich capacity for operating in the world of symbols and metaphor. It seems noteworthy that all of her questions were backward looking versus forward, which indicates a desire to understand, at a conscious level, what she had intuited after her walk.

What is clear to me is that Navi has a highly developed skill set for self-reflection and is no stranger to silent introspection. She displayed a deep awareness of her own preferences and what she feels is good for herself with regard to her educational decision making. Victor and Edith Turner assert, "The mystical dimension of pilgrimage, whether experienced on pilgrimage to particular sites or through a personal inner journey, involves confronting the self at a deeper level..."[49] Navi revealed precisely that to which the Turners point: the capacity for a deep encounter with self. Although Navi is a rare young person in her level of self-awareness, she too gained insights from her experience in the labyrinth. In fact, this is the point of such exercises: anyone can learn something from the silent

---

49   Turner and Turner, xi.

moving meditation that is the labyrinth, regardless of where they might be in their growth as an individual.

Loss and Lost Converge

The universal theme of loss, which arises as a result of the nature of the signature disorientation of the labyrinthine switchbacks, surfaces in the conversations I had with many students at Rabun Gap. "Did you feel like you were lost?" I asked.

"Yeah, for a little bit," one student said.

"How did that feel?"

"Not good."

"How does the unknown feel?"

"Scary, stressful. It's an ambiguous experience. I just had to go with it."

"Did you know where you were going?"

"We could see where we were going; it's not like we could get lost in it."

"But with big gigantic walls," another student added, "you'd always be wondering if there ever was an end and how much longer it would take."

Another commented, "I was thinking: 'What's happening?' Many people think they're going the wrong way."

A few more students arrived at the center and simply walked out without retracing their steps. "We were just focused on finishing," they told me when I asked why they did this. "It seemed longer going in, but you know it's a labyrinth, not a maze, so you know you won't get lost." Students were making connections with the journey and seemed to be overcoming concerns about getting truly lost in the labyrinth. They were confronting the possibility and moving through the fear instead.

A student confided, "I remember thinking on the bus ride over here, 'Oh, yay, something besides Naviance telling me what kind of person I am.'" Harkening back to Karasek's demand/control model and Gray's reflections on the locus of control relating to unhappiness, one can see that this student's comment might reflect the disillusionment of a computer program being able to "tell" a student who they are. Like Dr. Flummerfelt observed earlier, who a person is, their sense of self, must come from within one's center. In short, one's knowledge of themselves must originate in the practice of self-centering. Therefore, this exercise, walking the labyrinth, was precisely the activity that could shift the external locus to an internal locus of control.

Deep Peace

When I ask a group of students for their impressions after a labyrinth walk, the first words I usually hear are about how peaceful and quiet the experience is. "Quiet. Reflection. Repetitive," said one girl. "The Minotaur represents you leaving your doubt behind. The things that are nagging you."

A college guidance counselor contributed:

> It gets crazier and crazier as you go through the college process. I just sat with one senior who has several choices and is very confused. I told him to go be by himself and meditate and get his mind in the decision. Consider each college and think what would I be missing if I chose it. You need space and quiet and you have to search for that knowledge.

She continued, "You have to learn when to be quiet or still. Sometimes you just need to tell yourself, 'It's all going to be OK.'"

I asked her to describe the labyrinth in one word, and she said, "Uncomplicated! Because you know you're going to walk in and you're going to walk out and you're not going to hit any dead ends."

"How many things in your day are uncomplicated?" I asked.

"Not many." She laughed. "I thought about it, like long car rides at home. I didn't really resolve anything, but it gave me the time… I'm still stuck in school mode and it's hard to detach yourself from whatever is going on." This further confirms my conviction that the labyrinth is both a place of quiet and the liminal sacred space where distractions dissipate.

As I invited students to share the sensations they experienced while walking, one student shared, "I was kinda wondering what everyone else was thinking. I saw a butterfly." I had to admit that I too noticed some shamrocks growing when I sat in the center of the labyrinth as I walked it with them. We agreed that we were taking in, noticing, much more of the world as we walked. It seems obvious, perhaps, that the absence of cell phones and other technology contribute to awakening us to the minute details around us, but the experience itself also encourages inner silence, focus. The power of perception relative to rumination also emerged as a theme in our question and answer period.

Many definitions of mindfulness include precisely this: perception of the world rather than rumination about the world, which amounts to what might be called pre-thought, or the capacity to make decisions based more on unclouded unconscious processes rather than via traditional rational processing. There exists, then, an intuitive, leaping process rather than a strictly linear one that arises because of proceeding mindfully: in a word, insight. And this insight may be due to the impact that the twisting, turning path has on the brain hemispheres coming into balance, as we will see in the chapters that follow.

Inadequacy, Patience, and Memory

Some of the students I met at Rabun Gap were concerned with a feeling of inadequacy. One said to a staff member, "You assume we're going to find a good college that fits us, but there's always going to be a better one that I didn't find or I didn't get into... I'm not good enough for the best place so I have to settle for the second-best place." Although on the surface this assertion seems about fear of missing out, the student obviously feels inadequate to achieve even his own notion of the best fit for him regarding a college choice. In fact, many students are preoccupied with the notion of a wrong choice because the black or white narrative that is the current paradigm so has a lock on them that they struggle to escape the notion of a linear life and cannot completely accept the new paradigm I am suggesting we adopt when making college choices: that life is about making personal choices within a dynamic process of being. Indeed, many students begin to question what the college process is doing to their sense of self even before they are exposed to the alternative paradigm.

Another student railed against the application process: "It doesn't make you feel like yourself any more. You get shrunk down to two dimensions." It struck me then that these students were pushing back against any practices that contrive to reduce the individual to a set of numbers and canned categorical descriptors, metrics. In some cases, the labyrinth walk, this three-dimensional kinesthetic experience, brought these feelings to the surface; but in others, the experience simply afforded them a place and situation where they felt comfortable verbalizing these opinions. In either case, the labyrinth served to prompt a pause to weigh their thoughts and feelings on the matter.

Another common refrain was that of patience with the repetition:

"Maybe the Minotaur stayed in the center of the labyrinth, not because he was lost but because he was tired of going around and around and around."

"Yeah, doing the same thing over and over and over."

"Perhaps the Minotaur kept missing the point and so had to go round and round until he confronted his own truth," I suggested. "This requires ample amounts of both tenacity and patience."

I polled the students: "What do you need in order to finish the labyrinth?"

"Patience," was the unanimous response. Many students called my attention to words carved into some of the stones that lined the labyrinth, and "Patience" was one of them.

"You could easily jump the rocks and go to the center. It wouldn't be the right way, but you could do it," said one student.

"Does the college process require patience?" I followed up.

"Yes, because you're not always going to get what you want." I could not tell if this comment reflected a sense of inadequacy or of mature acceptance of the truth, but the student continued, "I felt like, 'This round I'll get to the middle,' but I had another round and another round… It happened to go near the center, but not yet." I interpreted this to mean that the student was approaching the concept of acceptance of outcomes beyond her control, acceptance of the fact that, if her first choices did not pan out, she'd need to exercise patience to keep her frustration under some control so she did not give up, but she had not yet achieved that idea consciously.

For her, this stage in the walk seemed to symbolize: "You are going to have to go back, not from square one but maybe square two. Restart. You think you're getting to the center, but you'll have to keep going."

"You do all that work to get to the center," said another student. "It's so far, when you get started… It takes so much longer than expected."

Others agreed: "I kept thinking… If I ran, I could do it faster."

Students were obviously making the connection between the walk and what it symbolizes within the context of that walk: the application process. The faster they complete the work, some were thinking, the less time they must endure in that liminal space and the unknown. They also were in the process of discovering that, like the walk, there are no shortcuts. This did not keep them from wanting one, however. "I found myself wanting to stray a lot. I could take a shortcut and go play in the creek."

This tension between wanting to speed up the process and understanding the value of slowing down is one that has surfaced before in previous chapters. The pace of the labyrinth, but also the college process and life itself for these students, is an excellent prompt for reflection post-walk. Pace within the labyrinth, that is, becomes a symbolic enactment of both slowing down in life and the necessary rate at which one should proceed with big decisions: deliberately and from the center of one's self. However, the deliberateness called upon by intentional labyrinth walkers inherently prompts a consciousness of, and discomfort with, the old paradigm, which encourages uncenteredness and speed. If they develop the intuitive ability to embrace the unknown and their discomfort overall, the path feels less like a burden to overcome and more like a quest within which opportunities abound.

Jan Flaska, a Deerfield Academy faculty member, spoke at the 2013 Association of Boarding Schools (TABS) conference about the fact that anyone can balance a bicycle pedaling fast, but only a disciplined rider can pedal slowly and maintain balance.[50] The walkers of the labyrinth also become more in touch with their surroundings when they are not rushing, as evidenced by the student who spotted a butterfly. Being more aware of one's surroundings makes the journey, the college application process, not only less stressful but more of an exercise in, and product of, mindfulness.

Another common theme that resonated among the Rabun Gap students was that of recalling childhood memories as we walked the labyrinth. One girl remarked how the walk reminded her of "being a little kid again. We went to a horse camp that had a little stone labyrinth, and the creek... I used to look for salamanders, but I don't get to do that anymore. Instead, I always have homework. That sucks."

Another student shared, "These picnic tables reminded me of my family and how, when it was nice out, we would just go outside and eat, but it's like I can't even do that anymore. I can go outside... and study."

These comments indicate a longing for the playful, unstructured time of self-exploration and intrinsic goals from their youth, and they also represent a palpable push back against extrinsic goals such as assignment deadlines, busy work, and homework. "There's

50   *The Association of Boarding Schools* (TABS) 2014 Conference, Boston, MA, session entitled "The Wisdom of Silence" by Jan Flaska.

constant pressure," I heard from one student. "Always got something to do."

"Do you think labyrinth walking would be beneficial to release stress?" I asked then.

The student replied, "You asked us to think of the college process... It reminded me more of what I was forgetting than the college process. I remembered childhood memories. They want us to focus so much on college we don't remember the everyday things we used to do, and walking just sparked memories from childhood."

This was a profound conversation for me, as I connected it to Gray's work on childhood play, which posits:

> My hypothesis is that the generational increase in externality, extrinsic goals, anxiety, and depression are all caused largely by the decline, over that same period, in opportunities for free play and the increased time and weight given to schooling.[51]

This decrease in play was certainly on the minds these participants, who correlate that loss directly with the overemphasis on education as the only goal of their current lives. These students are told how important the college decision is, but they repeatedly articulated that their sense of this emphasis on nothing but their education, and as a means to an end as adults, a career, grossly skews their lives.

Great Expectations

"I don't like to think about college very much because, where I want to go and where I will probably go, is a tough situation. I realize

---

51   Gray, 3.

that I have to localize. Financial reasons." This is not the first time I heard a student coming to terms with managing their expectations because of college costs. However, I was struck by how many more students at Rabun Gap noted finances as being a key attribute in their college selection process compared with the St. Andrew's students. The geographic location relative to socio-economic factors are no doubt at play here, but consider the worry families face who don't have the financial wherewithal to send their child to any boarding/prep school, regardless of geographic location relative to socio-economic factors, prior to college.

The reality of students' aspirations relative to limitations, whether financial or achievement related or geographic, can all be addressed in a labyrinth walk. The labyrinth experience, that is, is not limited to just a choice of college when all choices are on the table. Students can come to terms with external limitations and find peace and centeredness in their decision. In other words, the walk is not just about choice but also about acceptance.

When viewed through the lens of the paradigm I am suggesting, that of the college search process as a sacred journey, much more agency is accessible to the student, not just to choose a destination, but to accept that the choices they have are limited. Students can permit themselves to experience the college process as a dynamic journey and not exclusively as an end in both regards: this school and not that one for personal reasons, but also this school and not that one for reasons not within their control.

CHAPTER SEVEN

Lost and Found Faith: Chronicles of the Upper Room Spiritual Center

The final research group consisted only of adults, and this group walked the labyrinth without any overt direction regarding their path as I gave to the college-bound students. The ensuing discussion, much of which I will include below in narrative excerpts, waxed especially spiritual in topic and nature. I include them here to expand the scope of what is possible when using the labyrinth as a tool of spiritual/psychological development but also to enlarge the context for the decision students face regarding college and how adult stakeholders, especially parents' expectations, can amplify the stressors at the time of application and for decades to follow.

Those participants further along in their paths were more likely to see connections between their life-decisions and their motivations for these choices—desire for love, appreciation, status, self-worth—concepts and connections much harder for younger students to follow and to understand fully. With this group, I pivoted for the purposes of calling on adults to reflect back on college, and the result was a fecund discussion that makes what students discussed herein face a prolepsis for the reader, foreshadowing the results of unresolved issues surrounding externalizing the college process. There were also some delightful realizations about faith and family systems.

On that spring day in mid-May, Chrissy and Doug and Brenna, a former client of my practice, converged on the outdoor labyrinth at the Upper Room Spiritual Center in Neptune, New Jersey. The outdoor labyrinth is built in the Chartres model, made of gray slate stones, jagged on the edges and inlaid in the ground, the roseate center fashioned of neatly-fitted red paver stones.

At the beginning of the session, I said precious little to my guests about the labyrinth, simply inviting them to enter and walk at their own pace. Over a long lunch inside the center, we debriefed. I started us off by asking, as I did at both St. Andrew's and Rabun Gap, what their initial reactions were. What thoughts or words had percolated to the surface for them?

Chrissy began:

> I felt safe and secure in the labyrinth. I had the sensation that I'm in one place, but I keep moving. The view is different at every turn. I didn't have to worry where I was going because the path was laid out and I could appreciate the view. It was a reminder: don't be anxious about where we're going. We don't know the big picture. Don't try to plan so much as trust.

Doug agreed and continued:

> God puts you on a journey and sometimes you don't know where that journey will lead. When you go through a death in the family or loss, you may feel that God has

abandoned you, but He is really there for you. He puts people in your life for a reason. Friends and family... He put my wife and kids in my life. Good friends are there through thick and thin. When my dad died, my friend was always there for me. My other good friend walked me through the process of grieving, bringing me with my wife to the place where we felt secure that God is still with you. In the labyrinth, you want to see the end of the path, but you can't see it, you want to...we want our own path. But God has a path for us, which can be different from the original path we thought we were on. I learned to let go and go with the plan that God has... and I will tell you it is very difficult.

I paused then before commenting on the personal significance of the labyrinth we had walked—it was dedicated to the memory of my father's college roommate—and now here I was, listening to my research participants bring up loss of loved ones immediately in our debrief. I remarked that, in my practice, I have encountered some students who seem to exhibit an increased comfort and resilience around the chaos created by life transitions when they have experienced loss themselves.

Brenna responded:

Fashion design was the path I wanted to take. I applied to FIT [Fashion Institute of Technology] and put all my eggs in one basket. Of course, getting my rejection letter in the mail, I was so upset. My mom reminded me of Jeremiah 29:11: "For behold the plans I have for you says the Lord, plans to prosper you and not to harm you.

Plans to give you a hope and a future." It was very comforting. Not getting in and attending community college allowed me time to discover what I really wanted to do. Later I received a rejection letter from Kenyon, and all of those emotions resurfaced. I like feeling settled; I don't like the feeling of being vulnerable. Not seeing the path hinders me more than I can trust it. I focus on the negative of something not working out...self-doubt?... versus the positive. When I was accepted with a scholarship to Fordham, I seized the opportunity instantly.

Chrissy:

It's been ten years since my mother died. We had to go through it together as a family, and because we all grieved differently, our family totally disintegrated. So we had a double loss: loss of my mom and loss of family. We didn't have a family anymore. We are very much starting to come back together, really by the grace of God... We are doing a book group discussion over the phone from all corners of the country and this book we are discussing says, "All we can give God is our trust. That's all we can give Him... Which is really accepting His love." My one sister struggles: "I just want to know. Am I going to get married, and am I going to have kids?" It's just so hard not knowing. The book keeps saying, Jesus, I trust in you. Jesus seems to be saying, "I'll do everything else. If you trust me, I'll move mountains" It's so hard to trust. A week later, my sister called me and told me she was pregnant. She said, "I wasted all that time worrying. Why didn't I just trust?" I believe that what is good for your salvation, God will provide. Trust God to give that. He'll provide these opportunities. He'll never be lacking in those. Put it in the hands of the Lord. All He wants is our trust.

Brenna went next:

My maternal grandmother, Rose, passed away last summer. If I had not been at Brookdale, I couldn't have helped my mom. The sign that always reminded my mom of her mother was a yellow rose. After she passed, my parents went to a restaurant, and all the tables had yellow roses on them. A month after my grandmother's death, the phone rang and Care One King James came up on the caller ID. This was the nursing home my grandmother had been in. When my grandmother was alive, my mother always said a prayer when she had seen the call coming from the nursing home. "God keep them safe," she would say. Before her illness, when my grandmother was out, she would always call and let the phone ring once when she returned home to let my mother know that she had returned home safely. On that day, the phone rang from Care One King James, and there was no one on the other end. My mother began to cry. I walked in at that moment, having left my wallet at home, and it was just after the phone had rung. We took this as a sign from my grandmother. Even today, when I walked in for lunch, there are yellow roses on each table here at the Upper Room.

Doug was next:

> It was only eight weeks; lung cancer took my father
> that fast. He had been retired for just over a year. My
> brother, my mother, and myself were in the hospital
> room at Sloan Kettering Memorial Hospital when my
> father said, "Don't worry, God is with me." We were
> all shocked at this comment and the peace that accom-
> panied it. You realize in life, especially in our commu-
> nity, that money, wealth, and prestige become the most
> important measures of success. After my father retired,
> when he would call to check on the business, he would
> ask about how the people were doing, not how the
> bank was doing. He cared about the people, helping
> people, not simply the bottom line. After my father's
> death, when I was still working at the bank, I remember
> picking up the phone and dialing his extension out of
> habit… And then thinking, now to talk to him I don't
> even have to dial. At first it was very hard: "God why
> did you take away one of my best friends?" But that was
> the path he needed to go.

I explained to the three of them that I tried not to say too
much about the labyrinth experience prior to the walk, so as not to
influence their experiences. Brenna then admitted that she didn't
realize that the experience could be something spiritual. She had
envisioned a maze. I told the participants that, at the outset of my
research, I too used the terms interchangeably but soon learned
that the labyrinth offers only one path rather than trying to trick the
walker with dead ends and wrong turns. In that way, I observed, it is
an apt microcosm for life: you never have to turn back with regret.

I then noted that this difference between a maze and labyrinth is also representative of the failure of the current college admissions paradigm. As if in a maze, when the student believes there is only one possible successful outcome, he or she believes attaining admission to his/her first-choice college for its perceived cache and the empty promise of security that name is believed to deliver, any twist in the road, let alone outright obstacle, will be viewed as failure, or a risk to that outcome, and so these twists in the road are to be avoided at all costs. This fear of failure that is the hallmark of the current paradigm amounts to a psychological stranglehold on young adults, and we have not yet witnessed the full extent of the mental health impacts of this paradigm.

I then shared my own experiences with that day's walk. At one point, I was convinced I had no idea where I was but then realized that I was quite close to the center of the labyrinth. I admitted that I had been defining my walk and myself in relation to how close I believed I was to the center. Ironically, when I felt most vulnerable, I felt closer to God. As I began to relinquish the notion that the center is not the goal, I found that I had arrived. Once again, the theme of losing oneself to find oneself was apparent.

Chrissy replied:

> One example of this is a friend of mine who lost a child quite shortly after birth. She's never felt so close to God, she says. Sometimes she says she misses that intimacy, knowing that God is so close. That rocky ground can have a comforting element as well. She often says, "I have a foot in heaven because you are always where your children are." I find comfort in that because I have someone so close to me who is there [Chrissy's mother].

They are with Jesus, and he is everywhere. I am also comforted because I lost several children through miscarriage, and I like to think that there is a unique combination of my husband and me that my mom can experience in heaven.

Doug added:

God puts you on a path so that you can try to figure out some of the mysteries in your life. If I knew beforehand the challenges I would have to go through, I don't know if I would have signed on the dotted line. If you knew what was coming ahead, there's anxiety in that too. God doesn't want to overwhelm us.

While the labyrinth is a meditation tool with no concrete ties to any particular faith or religious belief, listening to the more-devout participants at the Upper Room research event reminded me of the Christian students' responses at St. Andrew's School. Many reported in their questionnaires that they trust that God has a plan for their lives. This is why, in moments of crisis, the labyrinth can be such a powerful and healing tool; walking it acknowledges that continuing on the path is indeed the only way forward.

These participants' assertions about faith in God's will/plan are obviously Christian in their overall perspective, but there are also secular interpretations of this same notion of acceptance. The labyrinth is helpful in simulating the experience of accepting what comes one's way and moving on from there, regardless of one's religious orientation or lack thereof. In her book *Getting Over Not Getting In*, Allison Singh draws from her own experience of being rejected from her "dream school" and offers insights and advice about not taking these somewhat arbitrary decisions personally. Perhaps it is the 180-degree blind turns in the labyrinth that help walkers to accept change or disappointment and to just keep their forward momentum, but in any event, walking the labyrinth teaches a tempered, calm resilience and grit in the face of changes outside of one's control.

"I must admit that I needed that path more than anyone," I confessed to the group. I too had been an Ivy undergraduate reject. I later attended two Ivy and world-class institutions (Yale and Oxford) but struggled for years with feelings of being "less-than" because I had not achieved entrance into my first-choice school. I told them that this reaction raises a larger question: who are you when you do not get what you want? Who are you when you don't get what you feel you merit or deserve? The labyrinth discipline helps to hush our worldly perceptions in exchange for increased internal clarity, and, while I was disappointed, I realized that my disappointment really stemmed from the expectations that others' had placed on me: that I would be "something" if I had been admitted that my parents would have "won" the parenting olympics, which results in the zero-sum consequence of feeling like "nothing" if not.

The labyrinth has repeatedly sensitized me to how rushed and hurried my life is. I'm often lacking the appreciation of looking up from the path that is my daily life. I shared with the group that I saw a blue jay today, and that I was listening. I noticed Brenna walking on certain stones and remembered a student from St. Andrew's School who had entered into a meditative mood by focusing on one step at a time in a pattern with the stones that constructed the path.

I also revealed how very acutely aware of how broken, how imperfect I am. I was observing the fractured fragments of the slate which I knew represented my life as a whole, as all those broken and many colored bits converged representing all of my root sins, namely my self-centeredness. What would this labyrinth look like if it were all paved, I thought, if I allowed God to be God and to heal me? Then an image came to me: the whole path paved and united.

Success and Self-Worth

As he discussed in our debrief, in 2000, Doug's father died of lung cancer. His father was the former chairman of a large New York City investment bank. Afterwards, Doug had to return to his loved ones and pick up where he left off in his career. He shared this:

> People get caught up in the money the power and put God on the back burner. Being in the area of compliance, I met a lot of people who breached ethics: wired money through their own accounts, sent customer statements to their home to take their book of business to another firm. They had gotten away from helping others. They consider their relationship with God as, "When I need your help, I'll call, but until then, I can do it myself." Money and power skews your view of the world. My father consistently said always to put God first. He didn't live in excess, and did the lawn as his therapy. As the Chairman, he had 165,000 people looking to him for answers. Yet, my mother observed that he slept extremely well. He had his values, the core values of the company, and tried his best—and that's all God is asking you for. Success gets confused with "things". In our society, we judge people in their success by their possessions.

How is this any different from how we judge success with name-brand college acceptance?

I can imagine that growing up the son of a father who had achieved so much professionally must have placed pressure on Doug to be just as high achieving. That is why I was pleased that, although this group only had one recent college applicant, some of the same themes that emerged among the teens immediately following their labyrinth walks surfaced in our conversation—loss and the pressures of pleasing our parents. As Chrissy confided:

> We also had a very successful father who built a bank. We learned quickly to derive our self-worth from achievements. Now I am watching my dad with my own children. We grew up thinking that he loved our achievements and not us. I got into Penn, that's an achievement he could be proud of. My sister is a research oncologist, that's something he could be proud of. My younger sister has the hardest job of all of us. She works with addicted children and teens. But for him, that's not a success, an achievement, not prestigious enough. We are striving to appreciate our children and not for their achievements. We got all the wrong signals from our father. My mom had open arms, as if to say, "Your being makes me love you." God is now working in my dad's heart. It wasn't achievement that made us worthwhile. Society tells us you have to be this and this. What does society value? That value and self-worth come from the prestigious college, the brand recognition.

I added:

> To circle back, my mission is to help students see
> that their value and worth come from within. I rarely
> invoke the name of God in my context because it is a
> non-sectarian one. If I could gesture at this journey as
> a sacred journey, and help them explore who they are,
> their unique gifts and skills, because we are all endowed
> with different gifts, how would you suggest I do that?
> I try to present the possibility of college as a journey
> that doesn't have a right choice or else you failed. I try
> to emphasize a perspective within which admission out-
> comes are less self judgmental, to communicate "you're
> valued because you are loved by God" without being so
> overtly religious.

Doug replied:

> I know. My daughter thinks it's Duke or nothing. She
> already knows she wants to go into the biomedical field.
> I only did one internship in college. But before that
> internship, I was a lifeguard. I had no idea what field
> I wanted to go into. So many young people are decid-
> ing so early. I don't want her to think that this selection
> is the be-all and end-all of your life. But at seventeen,
> eighteen, it seems like it is the defining moment.

Brenna suggested:

> High school nurtures this concept, but I explored my
> ultimate career direction through writing a research

paper on it. Support her and continue to tell her that, if she changes her mind, it's OK. For certain personality types, it's very hard to admit you're wrong. Nobody could tell me differently. I'm a passionate person in general. I go after things 100%. I had to learn for myself that I didn't want fashion design.

I then shared my recent experience of being a finalist in the job search:

I faced it myself, this black or white thinking, this wanting, when I started to dream of this position. It was painful to be in that limbo: do I give myself permission to dream it? My husband would ask, "Have you heard from…" It was so painful. Every point of contact made it more painful. I then prayed for relinquishment: "Take it away if it's not in your will." But when I found out I wasn't selected for the position, I was feeling judged, a failure, rejected. It has amplified my compassionate response to my students. It was humbling.

Chrissy responded:

The most powerful tool against evil is humility. Evil can't do anything with humility. Pride and ego are clay in the enemy's hand. As a high-achieving student, never having experienced failure was a detriment to me spiritually. If there's no failure, you feel bullet-proof, entitled to receive everything you wish.

Doug shared:

> Failure is important to teach resilience and grit. Thomas
> Edison was told to find a trade because he was not smart
> enough to succeed in school. Lincoln lost eight elec-
> tions—how humiliating—but he didn't give up, think-
> ing "maybe politics is not what I'm meant for." Michael
> Jordan was told he wasn't good enough to make varsity.
> He made it look easy, but he would shoot all hours of the
> night. No one saw that part. The obstacle becomes the
> stepping stone if you let it, the motivation. Sometimes
> we let the obstacle fall back on us.

I then thickened the questions by asking, "What happens
when you don't get what you want? Are access and affluence and
entitlement entangled?"

Chrissy replied:

> Those are the antithesis of humility, and so this [not
> getting the school they want] could be a great teaching
> lesson for students who are used to getting what they
> want, like *The Blessing of a Skinned Knee*. And studies con-
> sistently show that it really isn't the college you go to that
> matters, but what you do there that matters. At a recent
> conference, a couple from Ohio gave a presentation on
> how to parent affluent children. They were trying to
> stress that they have to own their own achievements.

> So they gave the scenario: Your child gets a C in math,
> what do you do? A) Don't worry. We're going to get

you a tutor five days a week. B) You're grounded. They advocated for the response: You got a C, how do you feel about that C? What are you going to do? How can I help support you? There was revolt in the audience. "My child doesn't have the leeway to get a C. They don't have the time. They have to compete with their peers." If children don't own it, they won't care. Always praise the work, the enjoyment, their improvement, not the achievement. They need to own the consequences of their achievements. Do not force them to be the producers of outcomes that you want. The truth is that parents adore being able to share their children's achievements. A parent shared that he felt he had won the parenting game when he could say that his child got into an Ivy League school, like bragging rights.

I asked Brenna, "If you had this labyrinth experience during the application process, might it have changed your experience?"

She replied:

It may have made it more of a spiritual journey. The process is so separated from being a spiritual journey that they are seen as opposites. You have to do what is most logical to get the best job to support yourself and have this salary to get this house…and be secure. From a spiritual perspective, the journey helped me to grow spiritually, however, because I was given the benefit of knowing failure. I am so grateful that I had the space and time to explore this and have my faith perspective validated.

The concept of entitlement—and the fear, reality, and blessing of rejection—are all themes that emerged that day just as they did during the other research days at St. Andrew's and Rabun Gap. Also notable was the emergence of the connection between the definition of success and attaching one's self-esteem and worthiness of being loved to college admissions outcomes. For example, Chrissy revealed she had been accepted into the University of Pennsylvania, and that it was an accomplishment in which her father could take pride. Imagine an adult woman speaking so thoughtfully and honestly about how much she wanted to achieve in order to earn love and how much she intuited that her father loved her achievements more than he loved her! She was simultaneously forty-one and seventeen again as she spoke of this experience. This is why time in a labyrinth is important throughout life: while our perceptions and perspective may grow over time, wounds can remain with us well into adulthood. Time to reflect in silence, whether in the labyrinth or in nature, on a retreat or in contemplation, helps the seeker to accept and even embrace the path they are on; and it is a valuable tool for attenuating the outer, more worldly measures of success in favor of exploring inner peace. As the Catholic saint, Francis de Sales, writes, "Never be in a hurry; do everything quietly and with a calm spirit. Do not lose your inner peace for anything whatsoever, even if your whole world seems upset."

In the Upper Room Spiritual Center labyrinth debriefing conversation that day, the concept of loss of a loved one came up without prompting. Clearly, the labyrinth elicited this openness to share about these profound losses. This small group spoke openly about God's role in their personal experiences of loss, which was a novel result, distinct from the other contexts of my research. This was perhaps a direct result of the faith lives of those attending, or maybe because of the perception of the Upper Room as a religious space.

While groups of high school students alone, absent adults as judges of student behavior or their effort, helped set the tone to allow for authentic emotions and feelings to surface, I also thoroughly enjoyed the ways in which the adults and Brenna interacted. Brenna was a client in the transfer process, and so a bit older than the traditional college applicant with whom I usually work (she was twenty). In fact, more mixed-age groups of stakeholders could enhance the richness of the college labyrinth dialogue for it is apparent that student and adult issues regarding the role of the college process overlap. The efficacy of the labyrinth to enable us to pause and reflect on the paradigm of the college application process as a dynamic journey of self awareness allows adults and students the freedom to define their perceptions of themselves outside of that bi-modal pattern of disgrace or triumph that is the current paradigm.

While the debriefing conversation at the Upper Room research experience was more overtly religious than at the two boarding schools, many of the same themes and refrains came up at all three sites. These postmodern nomads, of all ages and backgrounds, are interpreting the same human experience, the search for knowledge, that past generations may have taken for granted. For some I talked to, the stress of the college process dredged up older concerns and memories. For others, the process brought up adult concerns with work and family. Some invoked God while some did not, which only proves that walking the labyrinth is a meditative experience that can be used by anyone, regardless of their religious beliefs, to deepen a sense of purpose and pleasure in the adventure that is their life.

PART THREE: THE JOURNEY OUT

CHAPTER EIGHT

A Return to Love

Early on in my research, someone suggested that I omit the pilgrimage language from my research project entirely. They noted, "By not naming the process a 'pilgrimage,' you could create the space for it to bubble up from the storytelling." However, the notion of pilgrimage did not naturally emerge because, I discovered, the groups I researched were largely unfamiliar with the concept just as they seemed equally unexposed to the notion of the sacred. Nevertheless, those I observed during the labyrinth process seemed to know intimately what it meant to wander, to feel intense discomfort and vulnerability when faced with the unknown, which surfaced in the questionnaires and dialogue following the labyrinth walks. In the end, in choosing the faith-neutral labyrinth, students could relate to an epic journey full of twists and turns, one that fosters silence and reflection, one which allows them to access deep feelings, distant memories, and preferred futures. What walkers are engaged in, regardless of context and the language used to describe the experience/process, remains the same. To reiterate, the goal of introducing labyrinth experiences was to allow for silent exploration of self, for navigating the land betwixt and between notions of self and world that amounts to a journey of transformation, both intellectual and psychological, one with salubrious benefits for mind, body, and spirit.

I also observed many changes in myself and my own view of my consulting practice in a broader context. Ultimately, I want my work with teenagers to be of service to them as they process decisions that will define their futures. I learned the discipline of pausing, and I found an opportunity to practice the art of slowing down. I took copious notes following the walks, and I learned that, as an extrovert, having the opportunity to encounter quiet and clarify the overarching meta-themes of this practice was extremely helpful. It is difficult to see one's way out of a spiral and labyrinth (or a large-scale research undertaking) while one is in the midst of it. Because life has been so chock-full of demands—from running a business, to homeschooling my children, to completing my doctoral degree shortly after the birth of another child—I have recognized that, through the discipline of the labyrinth and the spiral model of action-reflection, spinning out of control is different than spiraling contemplatively. It is the difference between centrifugal and centripetal force. I sometimes feel like the former and so remind myself it can be the latter, and I can now better empathize with my clients' sense of not only being lost but bereft of bearings when unknown outcomes loom. It is obviously part of the human condition to become overwhelmed when many demands are placed on us, and the labyrinth process allows for a period of contextualization that leads us to perspective. In short, we are not simply defined by, or our futures predestined by, our actions, but rather, we are creatures capable of deep self-reflection and growth, cognitive and psychological and spiritual.

I've also come to realize that, if I am emanating freneticism because of my many tasks and responsibilities, it can be palpable to my clients and is certainly the opposite of what I intend for them to experience. I am a high-achieving striver, by definition, and so I have a tendency to welcome new challenges, and with them, the time-draining tasks required to achieve such goals. However, the labyrinth experience has reminded me that I must practice what I preach and treat each student's college process as a sacred journey, that I need to carve out the physical and psychological space necessary to emanate that calm lightheartedness of someone with whom they'd want to travel. While it may sound like a cliché, I learned as much from my research subjects as I hope they learned from our time together!

In theologian Stephen Pattison's "Some Straw for Bricks," he writes, "A real conversation is a living thing which evolves and changes."[52] This appeals to me in that it echoes the spiral in as much as it honors the act of conversation as organic. So it is with the action-reflection model, and so it has been with my research and my professional practice. "The important part of the conversation may be the silence, the disagreement or the lack of communication."[53] The very nature of the process of critical conversation creates and holds the space for the growth implicit in the descriptor "organic." We must think of the labyrinth and the college process as a space for transformation and enter that space willing to have our minds and hearts changed.

In spite of my personal discoveries and those of others in the field regarding the efficacy of the labyrinth process, however, it seems unlikely this will ever be accepted as part of the official process for the college application at Rabun Gap, given the race against time that most administrators experience. Educators and administrators

---

52 Stephen Pattison, "Some Straw for Bricks: A Basic Introduction to Theological Reflection," in *The Blackwell Reader in Pastoral and Practice Theology*, ed. James Woodward and Stephen Pattison (Hoboken, NJ: Wiley-Blackwell, 1999), 139.

53 Ibid., 140.

conceive of excellent ideas for student learning, but if the schedule will not yield, change is not made. I spoke to Reverend Jeffrey Reynolds, the chaplain at Rabun Gap, after our labyrinth experience, and he informed me that there had been no further discussion of incorporating the labyrinth into the college process. He wrote to me:

> As with most things, individual leadership is critical, and our team has been trained and motivated by the very calculated college industry within the Independent School world. My perception is that a labyrinth experience just hasn't developed the perceived influence required to become a highly valued tool in the college counselor's repertoire."

That is, the "very calculated college industry" of which he speaks is shaped by all of the stressors discussed at the beginning of this book. With stakes so high and the demands that the process be completed on a specific timeline, it appears unheard of to assign some of that time to process the impact of the journey itself. I know this to be true, as I have struggled to convey to parents in my practice the value of debriefing with their child after campus visits. They will ask, "Well, didn't you get anything done?" If all of the perceived value is on the action portion of the process, then the spiral devolves into a line extending from A to B with little opportunity to include, and no recognition of, the vital piece that is reflection.

Perhaps, akin to the third research experience, mixed generations of walkers (for example, parents and their high-school-aged children) might benefit from sharing the experience together. It may provide them with much-needed common text to foster dialogue about the college process. In fact, many parents report that their teenagers "shut down" when asked about college and offer no additional information about their feelings beyond one-word answers. It may also open up the lines of communication for applicants to express how parental behaviors may be exacerbating the pressure experienced by high schoolers. This shared experience might diminish some of the anxiety on both sides of the table.

How to Use the Labyrinth in the College Application Process

At Rabun Gap, I asked participants if this experience of labyrinth walking would be perceived as helpful to teens in the college process and, if so, how and at what point in the process. Here were the various responses:

"Well, if we really wanted to get technical, we could see it as a metaphor for the entire college journey in the first place. You go around and it's all good."

"At the end, an arrival ritual, like, 'You made it!'"

"Maybe use it to figure out what you want."

"Time to think is helpful with anything. College is a very stressful thing. Peace and quiet is valuable."

"Decision making lends itself to the labyrinth."

"In the beginning of the college process because applications seem complicated. Once you step into this, you just follow the path."

"The end to reflect back."

"In the labyrinth, I figured out what I want to do with my life, what I want to come from college."

"As human beings we are all on a journey, lots of twists and turns… Kind of like the college process."

"I've never really been bothered by due dates... I guess you really fire on both sides of the brain when you do something like this."

"In the beginning I was trying to figure out the pattern...but then I brought it back to the college process."

In this sampling of responses, we see students assigning value to the beginning and the end of the journey. One student mentioned creating a ritual. Perhaps she identifies the liminoid aspect of the process and desires it to be more liminal. We also see that at least one student had an insight regarding his life's direction. And another student had the epiphany that the labyrinth can be a metaphor for the college process!

While I have not made any formal recommendations to the college guidance professionals at Rabun Gap-Nacoochee School or St. Andrew's School, FL regarding incorporating the use of the labyrinth into the college process, it is my sincere hope that the positive experience that students enjoyed, and the fecund dialogue that manifested as a result, will encourage the staff to replicate this as part of the college search journey for their students and I remain grateful for the hospitality shown to me at both of these stellar independent schools.

The Burgeoning Field of Independent Educational Consulting

Perhaps the abiding practice of labyrinth walking, embedded so deeply in the traditions of the Catholic Church that it is literally embedded in the floors of many medieval cathedrals, is being rediscovered by the many faithful journeyers whom I have met precisely because humanity deeply desires an archetype of centering and reflection, regardless of religious beliefs. Indeed, there is circumstantial evidence indicating a correlation between the various periods of resurgence of the labyrinth archetype corresponding to chaotic historical time periods.

My broader context in this research is not based on a religious denomination, but a profession instead. The purpose of an independent educational consultant is to mentor students through their educational experience, especially when applying to colleges, and this perspective that we serve as a guide to help students find their way rather than a guru consrtuing some singular version of the path we devise for them is gaining traction among consultants. A company that designs software to track the college process recently renamed their venture from "My College Counselor Assistant" to "Guided Path," suggesting that, as the profession matures, the description of our work is becoming more journey-conscious, and hopefully, more apt.

Pilgrimage and Perambulation Revisited

When life's experiences challenge and disorient one's worldview (as in Tully's case, of losing his father) or being lost in the woods or in a theme park as a child (as both I and my daughter experienced), when truth no longer seems valid, one must seek to form a new kind of faith. It is often only through this disorganization and jumbling of what appears to be a fixed system that a new truth can emerge. So, whether a nomadic tribe wandering in the wilderness or a young person who has lost a parent and is trying to find his or her way in the college process, the status quo is disrupted—and perhaps it seems temporarily disintegrated.

Chaos in life is actually dynamic liminality that can either yield disorientation or opportunity, depending on one's past experiences as well as one's perspective. This is the great gift of the labyrinth—the offer of a way for safe passage. What will we find in the passage can only be answered by each individual voyager.

In pilgrimage, we lose our old selves on a journey toward something more expansive. St. Francis illustrates the beautiful way in which one can hold the paradoxes of mystery in tension. For example, in giving, we receive; in pardoning, we are pardoned. It is this kind of paradox that is at work in losing oneself and thereby subsequently finding oneself.

As a child, I became lost. As an adult, I lost a child in a crowded place. On 9/11, I lost at least a dozen people who had indelibly impacted my life. And if I look closely at these and consolidate them, I now recognize two important realities. The first: I have been living for the past decade with a frenzy of fear that I may not be long for this life, prompting an urgency to accomplish as much as possible. The second: in my urgency, I have compromised my inner peace and have been spinning wildly like a compass wheel when near a magnet.

Writing this book, labyrinth walking, small-group work with teens, and performing my own pilgrimage after my research experiences were complete (which I will detail in the next section) have helped me to restore order and balance in my life, and these activities have given me a desire to maintain my own inner peace and centeredness. In this way, I hope to maintain a contemplative disposition in all the circumstances of my life, one that flows from my unwavering convictions—my own Catholic faith and varied life experiences—from which the conditions of the world cannot separate me.

CHAPTER NINE

Labyrinth Lessons for Practitioners

I have here assembled some additional exercises as well as some probing reflection questions to encourage the paradigm shift toward a journeying mentality (some of which are adapted from Jill Geoffrion's *Praying the Labyrinth*) that you can use whether you are lucky enough to participate in a program that offers labyrinth walking or you need to seek out a labyrinth and design your own experience prior to and after the walk. These reflection questions can be created as journal entries (although there are some specific suggestions for this activity as well), printed on paper, cut into strips and selected from a hat, or listed as prompts on a shared Google doc for students to respond to or post.

The purpose of some of these questions is to give participants something to ponder prior to their labyrinth experience that guides them as they take time to assess and self-reflect. Some are questions to return to post-walk to open up discussion.

For Students

How might your experience be different if you approached it as a journey?

If you were to relax and trust the path you are on, what might you discover?

Do you need personal space or boundaries to help you focus on your goals?

Could you let go of outcomes and focus on the process? How might that free you to boldly pursue your dreams?

How does labyrinth walking diminish the outside noise and haste of your world? How might an inward focus change the way we see ourselves? Others? Our world?

How much of your self-worth comes from attaining external goods, goals, or praise?

Do the twists and turns in the labyrinth represent anything in your current life story?

How comfortable are you with a straight path? A curved path?

Who are you when you don't get what you want?

What are you being called to look at in your life? Is there anything that stands out as not in alignment with your values system?

What does authenticity feel like to you? How are you struggling to "be real" in the college application process?

Recall a memory when you felt completely at rest. Go there in your mind and body. Allow it to restore you now.

For Adult Stakeholders

How do you relate to your student/child/client/applicant as they travel on their quest?

What tools can you use to help your student/child/client/applicant find hope and joy?

Spinning is a way we describe being out of control. Spiraling, however, is a way to link action and reflection. Take some time to pause and reflect on where you are in the proverbial labyrinth of your personal, developmental, or professional life.

When in the last month/year/decade have you felt like you arrived at the center of the labyrinth?

Looking back, when might you have needed to shed or purge the mounting stress and burdens of your daily life? How might that have benefitted yourself, your spirit, your performance, your well-being, the people around you?

As I walk the labyrinth, how can each step bring me closer to becoming the best version of myself?

How has my energy changed, if at all, following a labyrinth walk? What signs in my body tell me change may have occurred?

For Participants Prone to Anxiety, Perhaps Manifested as Over-Thinking or Over-Analyzing

How has walking the labyrinth allowed you to dwell in, and focus on, the present moment?

How does worry and fear of the unknown interfere with your daily life? Your hopes and dreams?

What feelings do you wish to leave behind as you journey forward?

The Journey Journal

It can be helpful, in order to sensitize young people to the need to carve out interior space, to have them ask these questions of themselves prior to the walk and then to discuss their answers and how they feel about them post-walk:

Can I go somewhere or do an activity and not need my friends to join?

Do I feel empowered to make decisions without input?

Do I enjoy my own company?

How might my life change, if at all, if I had more silence in my life?

When, if ever, am I truly alone in the waking hours of my day?

What is the last mistake I made, big or small, and what, if anything, did I learn from it?

How have I incorporated that learning into my life?

How might I better take care of my body? Of my mental health and well-being?

What qualities in my friends or idols do I admire?

Who do I envision becoming in the future?

Have I ever given myself permission to say that it's okay to be unsure of something? If so, when?

EPILOGUE

A Journey In and Out

While I was researching the labyrinth experience with the hope of helping my clients better negotiate the application process within a cultural paradigm of high-stakes admissions that is not only stressful but ultimately a hindrance to making the right choice for students, I discovered my own sense of the process was, in fact, quite limited relative to the overall power of the labyrinth walk to slow us down, to center us within ourselves, and to prompt us to embrace the unknown proactively as an adventure—a process in its own right. I was aware that the labyrinth is used for many secular purposes, and I knew well its use in religion over centuries, but my understanding was intellectual and perhaps intuitive rather than experiential. And so I decided to take a pilgrimage of my own, albeit, still, as part of my research. What follows is more within the spiritual tradition of the labyrinth than the secular, but nevertheless, my experience connects to the psychological phenomena associated with the labyrinth and its beneficial effects.

As my research project came to a close, I journeyed to Chartres, France, a trip sponsored by Veriditas, an organization that trains labyrinth-workshop leaders and sponsors labyrinth construction worldwide. I believed the trip, which would include walking the famed labyrinth in the cathedral and learning more about it, would serve as a research opportunity, the culmination of my research project and nothing more. I was very much mistaken. Led by the Reverend Dr. Jill Kimberly Hartwell Geoffrion, labyrinth researcher and an expert on the Chartres Cathedral, the five-day journey was a faith pilgrimage to the heart of Marian theology—and it affected me greatly.

Dr. Geoffrion, an ordained Presbyterian minister, lectured in the morning about various installations in medieval cathedrals, especially the renowned stained glass windows, such as the North Rose, the architecture, and the relics housed in the cathedral. She then led us into the cathedral and we experienced these features by simulating ancient pilgrim rituals with time for meditative prayer.

On Monday, we circumambulated the cathedral, an ancient practice of pilgrims arriving at Chartres prior to entering the cathedral. One evening, we then entered the cathedral through the crypt, as pilgrims of old would have entered, and processed with a reliquary housing one of the three portions of the supposed veil of Mary, gifted to the cathedral by Charlemagne's grandson, Charles the Bald. What I thought would be a research trip became a surprisingly deep, enriching reconnection with my Roman Catholic with my Roman Catholic roots..

It was a time for personal transformation. While walking the labyrinth inlaid in the floor of the nave, I learned that, throughout the journey of life, there is a time for many different seasons. I learned that I cannot have everything all at once, that there is a time for sorrow and weeping and a time for joy and dancing.

I learned that life is not a race and to just slow down. In the labyrinth, I experienced the desire to dance and the joy of doing dance steps was only to be followed by the deep sadness that I do not dance more in my life currently.

Upon my return from this journey, this pilgrimage, I meditated on the fact that there is indeed a time for every season, and the most difficult of seasons are the dark ones. These are the times when we must do the difficult self-work of cultivating our own souls, of listening and looking deeply and confronting that which separates us from God's divine will for our lives. That work is real, and it is hard work. I know now that I can make changes to experience true freedom.

I have also endeavored to bring such changes to my work, indeed to the overall paradigm of the college search process, to do my part to take it from a black or white ordeal with only success, (as defined by the culture) as the goal and to transform it into a journey of self-discovery that just happens to include picking the best college for each individual student—and based on who they are and are becoming rather than a list of accomplishments—in the process.

The old paradigm consisting of zero-sum game, Machiavellian tactics to get ahead is detrimental because it is not only soul-crushing but failure fostering. The new paradigm consists of approaching times of transition, including the college process, as a sacred journey that benefits young people because it affirms the chaos inherent in transition and takes into account all of the opportunity that abounds therein. The labyrinth walk is an excellent tool to pause, quiet the mind, focus, become attentive and reflect. The steps involve designing mindful meditation opportunities to prompt dialogue not only regarding the journey of the individuals involved but regarding navigating the current paradigm by exploring how it is endangering the well-being of individuals and communities of individuals navigating these transitions, thereby squandering opportunities for self-development.

Ultimately, if the institutions on either end of the application process, high schools and colleges, are not able to recognize the need for a more student-centered approach to the college journey, then it is up to students and those who care for and guide them to provide that opportunity.

I began my journey with my exploration of the potential role of the labyrinth in the college application process, seeking a new implementation for a very old tool, and I, somewhat ironically, culminated my project by walking the largest and perhaps best known twelfth-century cathedral labyrinth, gleaning from it spiritual growth and renewal just as the ancient pilgrims had done! I now fervently appreciate that recognizing a space as sacred is intimately intertwined with the acknowledgment that each one of us is on a journey. So whether the journey is physical, psychological, overtly spiritual or simply metaphorical, the archetype of the labyrinth provides tremendous promise as a powerful tool to navigate change and to help us remain centered. As a Shaker hymn corroborates:

'Tis the gift to be simple, 'tis the gift to be free

'Tis the gift to come down where we ought to be,

And when we find ourselves in the place just right,

'Twill be in the valley of love and delight.

When true simplicity is gained,

To bow and to bend we shan't be ashamed,

To turn, turn will be our delight,

Till by turning, turning we come 'round right.[54]

Journey on in peace.

---

54 Joseph Brackett, "Simple Gifts" in *Joseph Brackett's Simple Gifts* by Roger Lee Hall, accessed November 2, 2014, http://americnamusicpreservation.com/shakermusicscholar. htm#shakermusicresearch.